NIST Special Publication 800-37
Revision 1

Guide for Applying the Risk Management Framework to Federal Information Systems

A Security Life Cycle Approach

**JOINT TASK FORCE
TRANSFORMATION INITIATIVE**

http://dx.doi.org/10.6028/NIST.SP.800-37r1

**National Institute of
Standards and Technology**
U.S. Department of Commerce

NIST Special Publication 800-37
Revision 1

Guide for Applying the Risk Management Framework to Federal Information Systems

A Security Life Cycle Approach

**JOINT TASK FORCE
TRANSFORMATION INITIATIVE**

*Computer Security Division
Information Technology Laboratory
National Institute of Standards and Technology*

http://dx.doi.org/10.6028/NIST.SP.800-37r1

February 2010
INCLUDES UPDATES AS OF 06-05-2014: PAGE IX

U.S. Department of Commerce
Gary Locke, Secretary

National Institute of Standards and Technology
Patrick D. Gallagher, Director

Authority

This publication has been developed by NIST to further its statutory responsibilities under the Federal Information Security Management Act (FISMA), Public Law (P.L.) 107-347. NIST is responsible for developing information security standards and guidelines, including minimum requirements for federal information systems, but such standards and guidelines shall not apply to national security systems without the express approval of appropriate federal officials exercising policy authority over such systems. This guideline is consistent with the requirements of the Office of Management and Budget (OMB) Circular A-130, Section 8b(3), *Securing Agency Information Systems*, as analyzed in Circular A-130, Appendix IV: *Analysis of Key Sections*. Supplemental information is provided in Circular A-130, Appendix III, *Security of Federal Automated Information Resources*.

Nothing in this publication should be taken to contradict the standards and guidelines made mandatory and binding on federal agencies by the Secretary of Commerce under statutory authority. Nor should these guidelines be interpreted as altering or superseding the existing authorities of the Secretary of Commerce, Director of the OMB, or any other federal official. This publication may be used by nongovernmental organizations on a voluntary basis and is not subject to copyright in the United States. Attribution would, however, be appreciated by NIST.

National Institute of Standards and Technology Special Publication 800-37 Revision 1
Natl. Inst. Stand. Technol. Spec. Publ. 800-37 Revision 1, 102 pages (February 2010)
CODEN: NSPUE2

This publication is available free of charge from: http://dx.doi.org/10.6028/NIST.SP.800-37r1

Certain commercial entities, equipment, or materials may be identified in this document in order to describe an experimental procedure or concept adequately. Such identification is not intended to imply recommendation or endorsement by NIST, nor is it intended to imply that the entities, materials, or equipment are necessarily the best available for the purpose.

There may be references in this publication to other publications currently under development by NIST in accordance with its assigned statutory responsibilities. The information in this publication, including concepts, practices, and methodologies, may be used by federal agencies even before the completion of such companion publications. Thus, until each publication is completed, current requirements, guidelines, and procedures, where they exist, remain operative. For planning and transition purposes, federal agencies may wish to closely follow the development of these new publications by NIST.

Organizations are encouraged to review draft publications during the designated public comment periods and provide feedback to NIST. Computer Security Division publications are available at http://csrc.nist.gov/publications.

Comments on this publication may be submitted to:

National Institute of Standards and Technology
Attn: Computer Security Division, Information Technology Laboratory
100 Bureau Drive (Mail Stop 8930) Gaithersburg, MD 20899-8930
Electronic Mail: sec-cert@nist.gov

Reports on Computer Systems Technology

The Information Technology Laboratory (ITL) at the National Institute of Standards and Technology (NIST) promotes the U.S. economy and public welfare by providing technical leadership for the Nation's measurement and standards infrastructure. ITL develops tests, test methods, reference data, proof of concept implementations, and technical analyses to advance the development and productive use of information technology. ITL's responsibilities include the development of management, administrative, technical, and physical standards and guidelines for the cost-effective security and privacy of other than national security-related information in federal information systems. The Special Publication 800-series reports on ITL's research, guidelines, and outreach efforts in information system security, and its collaborative activities with industry, government, and academic organizations.

Abstract

This publication provides guidelines for applying the Risk Management Framework (RMF) to federal information systems. The six-step RMF includes security categorization, security control selection, security control implementation, security control assessment, information system authorization, and security control monitoring. The RMF promotes the concept of near real-time risk management and ongoing information system authorization through the implementation of robust continuous monitoring processes, provides senior leaders the necessary information to make cost-effective, risk-based decisions with regard to the organizational information systems supporting their core missions and business functions, and integrates information security into the enterprise architecture and system development life cycle. Applying the RMF within enterprises links risk management processes at the information system level to risk management processes at the organization level through a risk executive (function) and establishes lines of responsibility and accountability for security controls deployed within organizational information systems and inherited by those systems (i.e., common controls).

Keywords

Risk management, risk assessment, security authorization, security control, system development life cycle, Risk Management Framework, security control assessment, continuous monitoring, ongoing authorization, security categorization, security control selection, security plan, security assessment report, plan of action and milestones, security authorization package, authorization to operate, common control, information system owner/steward, senior information security officer, common control provider, authorizing official.

Compliance with NIST Standards and Guidelines

In accordance with the provisions of FISMA,[1] the Secretary of Commerce shall, on the basis of standards and guidelines developed by NIST, prescribe standards and guidelines pertaining to federal information systems. The Secretary shall make standards compulsory and binding to the extent determined necessary by the Secretary to improve the efficiency of operation or security of federal information systems. Standards prescribed shall include information security standards that provide minimum information security requirements and are otherwise necessary to improve the security of federal information and information systems.

- Federal Information Processing Standards (FIPS) are approved by the Secretary of Commerce and issued by NIST in accordance with FISMA. FIPS are compulsory and binding for federal agencies.[2] FISMA requires that federal agencies comply with these standards, and therefore, agencies may not waive their use.

- Special Publications (SPs) are developed and issued by NIST as recommendations and guidance documents. For other than national security programs and systems, federal agencies must follow those NIST Special Publications mandated in a Federal Information Processing Standard. FIPS 200 mandates the use of Special Publication 800-53, as amended. In addition, OMB policies (including OMB Reporting Instructions for FISMA and Agency Privacy Management) state that for other than national security programs and systems, federal agencies must follow certain specific NIST Special Publications.[3]

- Other security-related publications, including interagency reports (NISTIRs) and ITL Bulletins, provide technical and other information about NIST's activities. These publications are mandatory only when specified by OMB.

- Compliance schedules for NIST security standards and guidelines are established by OMB in policies, directives, or memoranda (e.g., annual FISMA Reporting Guidance).

---

[1] The E-Government Act (P.L. 107-347) recognizes the importance of information security to the economic and national security interests of the United States. Title III of the E-Government Act, entitled the Federal Information Security Management Act (FISMA), emphasizes the need for organizations to develop, document, and implement an organization-wide program to provide security for the information systems that support its operations and assets.

[2] The term *agency* is used in this publication in lieu of the more general term *organization* only in those circumstances where its usage is directly related to other source documents such as federal legislation or policy.

[3] While federal agencies are required to follow certain specific NIST Special Publications in accordance with OMB policy, there is flexibility in how agencies apply the guidance. Federal agencies apply the security concepts and principles articulated in the NIST Special Publications in accordance with and in the context of the agency's missions, business functions, and environment of operation. Consequently, the application of NIST guidance by federal agencies can result in different security solutions that are equally acceptable, compliant with the guidance, and meet the OMB definition of *adequate security* for federal information systems. Given the high priority of information sharing and transparency within the federal government, agencies also consider reciprocity in developing their information security solutions. When assessing federal agency compliance with NIST Special Publications, Inspectors General, evaluators, auditors, and assessors consider the intent of the security concepts and principles articulated within the specific guidance document and how the agency applied the guidance in the context of its mission/business responsibilities, operational environment, and unique organizational conditions.

Acknowledgements

This publication was developed by the *Joint Task Force Transformation Initiative* Interagency Working Group with representatives from the Civil, Defense, and Intelligence Communities in an ongoing effort to produce a unified information security framework for the federal government. The Project Leader, Ron Ross, from the National Institute of Standards and Technology, wishes to acknowledge and thank the senior leadership team from the U.S. Departments of Commerce and Defense, the Office of the Director of National Intelligence, the Committee on National Security Systems, and the members of the interagency working group whose dedicated efforts contributed significantly to the publication. The senior leadership team, working group members, and their organizational affiliations include:

U.S. Department of Defense

Cheryl J. Roby
Acting Assistant Secretary of Defense for Networks and Information Integration/ DoD Chief Information Officer

Gus Guissanie
Acting Deputy Assistant Secretary of Defense for Cyber, Identity, and Information Assurance

Dominic Cussatt
Senior Policy Advisor

Office of the Director of National Intelligence

Honorable Priscilla Guthrie
Intelligence Community Chief Information Officer

Sherrill Nicely
Deputy Intelligence Community Chief Information Officer

Mark J. Morrison
Deputy Associate Director of National Intelligence for IC Information Assurance

Roger Caslow
Lead, C&A Transformation

National Institute of Standards and Technology

Cita M. Furlani
Director, Information Technology Laboratory

William C. Barker
Chief, Computer Security Division

Ron Ross
FISMA Implementation Project Leader

Committee on National Security Systems

Cheryl J. Roby
Acting Chair, Committee on National Security Systems

Eustace D. King
CNSS Subcommittee Co-Chair (DoD)

William Hunteman
CNSS Subcommittee Co-Chair (DoE)

Joint Task Force Transformation Initiative Interagency Working Group

Ron Ross *NIST, JTF Leader*	Gary Stoneburner *Johns Hopkins APL*	Dominic Cussatt *Department of Defense*	Kelley Dempsey *NIST*
Marianne Swanson *NIST*	Jennifer Fabius Greene *MITRE Corporation*	Dorian Pappas *National Security Agency*	Arnold Johnson *NIST*
Stuart Katzke *Booz Allen Hamilton*	Peter Williams *Booz Allen Hamilton*	Peter Gouldmann *Department of State*	Christian Enloe *NIST*

In addition to the above acknowledgments, a special note of thanks goes to Peggy Himes and Elizabeth Lennon for their superb technical editing and administrative support. The authors also wish to recognize Beckie Bolton, Marshall Abrams, John Gilligan, Richard Graubart, Esten Porter, Karen Quigg, George Rogers, John Streufert, and Glenda Turner for their exceptional contributions in helping to improve the content of the publication. And finally, the authors gratefully acknowledge and appreciate the significant contributions from individuals and organizations in the public and private sectors, nationally and internationally, whose thoughtful and constructive comments improved the overall quality and usefulness of this publication.

DEVELOPING COMMON INFORMATION SECURITY FOUNDATIONS

COLLABORATION AMONG PUBLIC AND PRIVATE SECTOR ENTITIES

In developing standards and guidelines required by FISMA, NIST consults with other federal agencies and the private sector to improve information security, avoid unnecessary and costly duplication of effort, and ensure that its publications are complementary with the standards and guidelines employed for the protection of national security systems. In addition to a comprehensive public review and vetting process, NIST is collaborating with the Office of the Director of National Intelligence (ODNI), the Department of Defense (DoD), and the Committee on National Security Systems (CNSS) to establish a unified information security framework for the federal government. A common foundation for information security will provide the Civil, Defense, and Intelligence sectors of the federal government and their contractors, more cost-effective and consistent ways to manage information security-related risk to organizational operations and assets, individuals, other organizations, and the Nation. The unified framework will also provide a strong basis for reciprocal acceptance of authorization decisions and facilitate information sharing. NIST is also working with many public and private sector entities to establish mappings and relationships between the security standards and guidelines developed by NIST and the International Organization for Standardization and International Electrotechnical Commission (ISO/IEC).

Table of Contents

Prologue

"…Through the process of risk management, leaders must consider risk to US interests from adversaries using cyberspace to their advantage and from our own efforts to employ the global nature of cyberspace to achieve objectives in military, intelligence, and business operations… "

"…For operational plans development, the combination of threats, vulnerabilities, and impacts must be evaluated in order to identify important trends and decide where effort should be applied to eliminate or reduce threat capabilities; eliminate or reduce vulnerabilities; and assess, coordinate, and deconflict all cyberspace operations… "

"…Leaders at all levels are accountable for ensuring readiness and security to the same degree as in any other domain… "

-- THE NATIONAL STRATEGY FOR CYBERSPACE OPERATIONS
   OFFICE OF THE CHAIRMAN, JOINT CHIEFS OF STAFF, U.S. DEPARTMENT OF DEFENSE

Errata

The following changes have been incorporated into Special Publication 800-37, Revision 1. Errata updates include corrections, clarifications, or other minor changes in the publication that are either *editorial* or *substantive* in nature.

DATE	TYPE	CHANGE	PAGE
06-05-2014	Substantive	Added Abstract Section.	iii
06-05-2014	Substantive	Added Keywords Section.	iii
06-05-2014	Substantive	Added "The information system owner and information owner/steward consider results from the initial risk assessment as a part of the security categorization decision. The security categorization decision is consistent with the organization's risk management strategy to identify potential impact to mission/business functions resulting from the loss of confidentiality, integrity, and/or availability." to Task 1-1, Supplemental Guidance.	21
06-05-2014	Editorial	Moved "The results of the security categorization process influence the selection of appropriate security controls for the information system and also, where applicable, the minimum assurance requirements for that system." to the beginning of new paragraph 2, Task 1-1, Supplemental Guidance.	21
06-05-2014	Substantive	Changed "executive (function)" to "management strategy" in Task 1-1, Supplemental Guidance.	21
06-05-2014	Substantive	Deleted "concerning the risk management strategy for the organization" from Task 1-1, Supplemental Guidance.	21
06-05-2014	Editorial	Moved "The organization may consider decomposing the information system… into multiple subsystems to more efficiently and effectively allocate security controls to the system. One approach is to categorize each identified subsystem (including dynamic subsystems). Separately categorizing each subsystem does not change the overall categorization of the information system. Rather, it allows the constituent subsystems to receive a separate allocation of security controls from NIST Special Publication 800-53 instead of deploying higher-impact controls across every subsystem. Another approach is to bundle smaller subsystems into larger subsystems within the information system, categorize each of the aggregated subsystems, and allocate security controls to the subsystems, as appropriate. Security categorization information is documented in the system identification section of the security plan or included as an attachment to the plan." to end of Task 1-1, Supplemental Guidance.	21
06-05-2014	Substantive	Added "(informed by the initial risk assessment)" to Milestone Checkpoint #1.	23
06-05-2014	Substantive	Deleted "The security control selection process includes, as appropriate: (i) choosing a set of baseline security controls; (ii) tailoring the baseline security controls by applying scoping, parameterization, and compensating control guidance; (iii) supplementing the tailored baseline security controls, if necessary, with additional controls and/or control enhancements to address unique organizational needs based on a risk assessment (either formal or informal) and local conditions including environment of operation, organization-specific security requirements, specific threat information, cost-benefit analyses, or special circumstances; and (iv) specifying minimum assurance requirements, as appropriate. Organizations document in the security plan, the decisions (e.g., tailoring, supplementation, etc.) taken during the security control selection process, providing a sound rationale for those decisions." from Task 2-2, Supplemental Guidance, paragraph 1.	25

DATE	TYPE	CHANGE	PAGE
06-05-2014	Substantive	Added "After selecting the applicable security control baseline, organizations apply the tailoring process to align the controls more closely with the specific conditions within the organization (i.e., conditions related to organizational risk tolerance, missions/business functions, information systems, or environments of operation). The tailoring process includes: (i) identifying and designating common controls in initial security control baselines; (ii) applying scoping considerations to the remaining baseline security controls; (iii) selecting compensating security controls, if needed; (iv) assigning specific values to organization-defined security control parameters via explicit assignment and selection statements; (v) supplementing baselines with additional security controls and control enhancements, if needed; and (vi) providing additional specification information for control implementation, if needed. Organizations use risk assessments to inform and guide the tailoring process for organizational information systems and environments of operation. Threat data from risk assessments provide critical information on adversary capabilities, intent, and targeting that may affect organizational decisions regarding the selection of additional security controls, including the associated costs and benefits. Risk assessment results are also leveraged when identifying common controls to help determine if such controls available for inheritance meet the security requirements for the system and its environment of operation (including analyses for potential single points of failure)." to Task 2-2, Supplemental Guidance, paragraph 1.	25
06-05-2014	Substantive	Deleted "selected" from item (iii) in Task 2-3, Supplemental Guidance.	26
06-05-2014	Substantive	Deleted "selecting security controls to be monitored post deployment and for" from Task 2-3, Supplemental Guidance, paragraph 2.	26
06-05-2014	Substantive	Changed "of such monitoring" to "with which security controls are monitored post deployment" in Task 2-3, Supplemental Guidance, paragraph 2.	26
06-05-2014	Substantive	Changed "selection" to "frequency" in Task 2-3, Supplemental Guidance, paragraph 2.	26
06-05-2014	Substantive	Changed "are assessed as frequently as necessary consistent with the criticality of the function and capability of the monitoring tools" to "may require more frequent assessment" in Task 2-3, Supplemental Guidance, paragraph 2.	26
06-05-2014	Substantive	Deleted "selection of specific security controls to be monitored and the" from Task 2-3, Supplemental Guidance, paragraph 3.	26
06-05-2014	Substantive	Deleted "such" from Task 2-3, Supplemental Guidance, paragraph 3.	26
06-05-2014	Substantive	Added "NIST Special Publication 800-137 provides additional guidance on continuous monitoring and continuous monitoring strategies." to Task 2-3, Supplemental Guidance, paragraph 4.	26
06-05-2014	Editorial	Changed ";" to "," after 800-53 in Task 2-3, References.	26
06-05-2014	Substantive	Added "800-137" to Task 2-3, References.	26
06-05-2014	Substantive	Deleted "and supplemented" from Milestone Checkpoint #2.	27
06-05-2014	Substantive	Added "Early integration of information security requirements into the system development life cycle is the most cost-effective method for implementing the organizational risk management strategy at Tier 3." to Task 3-1, Supplemental Guidance, paragraph 1.	28
06-05-2014	Substantive	Added "Risk assessment may help inform decisions regarding the cost, benefit, and risk trade-offs in using one type of technology versus another for control implementation." to Task 3-1, Supplemental Guidance, paragraph 1.	28
06-05-2014	Substantive	Added "Risk assessment may help determine how gaps in protection needs between systems and common controls affect the overall risk associated with the system, and how to prioritize the need for compensating or supplementary controls to mitigate specific risks." to Task 3-1, Supplemental Guidance, paragraph 2.	28
06-05-2014	Editorial	Change "make" to "support" in Task 4-1, Supplemental Guidance, paragraph 2.	30

DATE	TYPE	CHANGE	PAGE
06-05-2014	Substantive	Added "or that are discovered post-development. Such weaknesses and deficiencies are potential vulnerabilities if exploitable by a threat source." to Task 4-4, Supplemental Guidance, paragraph 1.	32
06-05-2014	Substantive	Added "provide important information that" to Task 4-4, Supplemental Guidance, paragraph 1.	32
06-05-2014	Editorial	Change "facilitate" to "facilitates" in Task 4-4, Supplemental Guidance, paragraph 1.	32
06-05-2014	Substantive	Added ", based on an initial or updated assessment of risk," to Task 4-4, Supplemental Guidance, paragraph 1.	32
06-05-2014	Editorial	Moved "An updated assessment of risk (either formal or informal) based on the results of the findings produced during the security control assessment and any inputs from the risk executive (function), helps to determine the initial remediation actions and the prioritization of such actions." in Task 4-4, Supplemental Guidance, paragraph 1.	32
06-05-2014	Substantive	Added "the security control assessor reassesses" to Task 4-4, Supplemental Guidance, paragraph 1.	33
06-05-2014	Substantive	Deleted "are reassessed" from Task 4-4, Supplemental Guidance, paragraph 1.	33
06-05-2014	Substantive	Added "Did the assessor reassess the remediated controls for effectiveness to provide the authorization official with an unbiased, factual security assessment report on the weaknesses or deficiencies in the system?" to Milestone Checkpoint #4?	33
06-05-2014	Substantive	Changed "mitigation" to "response" in Task 5-3, Supplemental Guidance, paragraph 1.	35
06-05-2014	Substantive	Added "After risk determination, organizations can respond to risk in a variety of ways, including: (i) accepting risk; (ii) avoiding risk; (iii) mitigating risk; (iv) sharing risk; (v) transferring risk; or (vi) a combination of the above. Decisions on the most appropriate course of action for risk response include some form of prioritization. Some risks may be of greater concern than other risks. In that case, more resources may need to be directed at addressing higher-priority risks than at other lower-priority risks. This does not necessarily mean that the lower-priority risks are ignored. Rather, it could mean that fewer resources are directed at the lower-priority risks (at least initially), or that the lower-priority risks are addressed at a later time. A key part of the risk decision process is the recognition that regardless of the risk decision, there typically remains a degree of residual risk. Organizations determine acceptable degrees of residual risk based on organizational risk tolerance." to Task 5-3, Supplemental Guidance, paragraph 1.	35
06-05-2014	Editorial	Moved "Authorization termination dates are influenced by federal and/or organizational policies which may establish maximum authorization periods." to second paragraph in Task 5-4, Supplemental Guidance.	36
06-05-2014	Substantive	Deleted "For example, if the maximum authorization period for an information system is three years, then an organization establishes a continuous monitoring strategy for assessing a subset of the security controls employed within and inherited by the system during the authorization period. This strategy allows all security controls designated in the respective security plans to be assessed at least one time by the end of the three-year period. This also includes any common controls deployed external to organizational information systems." from Task 5-4, Supplemental Guidance, paragraph 3.	36
06-05-2014	Substantive	Added "As risk assessments are updated and refined, organizations use the results to modify security plans based on the most recent threat and vulnerability information available. Updated risk assessments provide a foundation for prioritizing/planning risk responses." to Task 6-1, Supplemental Guidance, paragraph 2.	38
06-05-2014	Substantive	Deleted "a selected subset of" from Task 6-2.	38

DATE	TYPE	CHANGE	PAGE
06-05-2014	Substantive	Deleted "Organizations assess all security controls employed within and inherited by the information system during the initial security authorization." from Task 6-2, Supplemental Guidance.	39
06-05-2014	Editorial	Added "(i.e., during continuous monitoring)" after "initial authorization" to Task 6-2, Supplemental Guidance.	39
06-05-2014	Substantive	Changed "a subset of the" to "all" in Task 6-2, Supplemental Guidance.	39
06-05-2014	Substantive	Added "employed within and inherited by the information system" to Task 6-2, Supplemental Guidance.	39
06-05-2014	Editorial	Deleted "during continuous monitoring" after "on an ongoing basis" from Task 6-2, Supplemental Guidance.	39
06-05-2014	Substantive	Deleted "selection of appropriate security controls to monitor and the" from Task 6-2, Supplemental Guidance.	39
06-05-2014	Editorial	Changed "are" to "is" in Task 6-2, Supplemental Guidance.	39
06-05-2014	Substantive	Added "in support of ongoing authorization and" to Task 6-2, Supplemental Guidance.	39
06-05-2014	Substantive	Added "800-137" to Task 6-2, References.	39
06-05-2014	Editorial	Changed "Publication" to "Publications" in Task 6-2, References.	39
06-05-2014	Editorial	Changed "Decommissioning" to "Disposal" in Task 6-7, Title.	41
06-05-2014	Editorial	Changed "decommissioning" to "disposal" in Task 6-7.	41
06-05-2014	Editorial	Changed "decommissioning" to "disposal" in Task 6-7, Supplemental Guidance, two instances.	41
06-05-2014	Substantive	Added "National Institute of Standards and Technology Special Publication 800-128, *Guide for Security-Focused Configuration Management of Information Systems*, August 2011." to Appendix A, References.	A-2
06-05-2014	Substantive	Added "National Institute of Standards and Technology Special Publication 800-137, *Information Security Continuous Monitoring for Federal Information Systems and Organizations*, September 2011." to Appendix A, References.	A-2
06-05-2014	Editorial	Added definition of "Continuous Monitoring" to Appendix B, Glossary.	B-3
06-05-2014	Editorial	Added definition of "Risk Assessor" to Appendix B, Glossary.	B-8
06-05-2014	Substantive	Added "and control enhancements" to Appendix D, Section D.13, paragraph 1.	D-7
06-05-2014	Substantive	Deleted "a selected subset of" from Appendix E, Task 6-2.	E-4
06-05-2014	Editorial	Changed "Decommissioning" to "Disposal" in Appendix E, Task 6-7, Title.	E-5
06-05-2014	Editorial	Changed "decommissioning" to "disposal" in Appendix E, Task 6-7.	E-5
06-05-2014	Substantive	Added "Organizations provide an official designation (including any approvals required) for information systems that have transitioned from initial authorization to operate into an ongoing authorization approach." to Appendix F, Section F.4, paragraph 1.	F-6
06-05-2014	Substantive	Changed "adequately mitigate;" to "effectively respond to" in Appendix F, Section F.4, paragraph 2.	F-6
06-05-2014	Editorial	Moved "Formal reauthorization actions occur at the discretion of the authorizing official in accordance with federal or organizational policy." from Appendix F, Section F.4, paragraph 2 to new Section F.5, Reauthorization, paragraph 1.	F-6
06-05-2014	Substantive	Deleted "If a formal reauthorization action is required, organizations maximize the use of security and risk-related information produced during the continuous monitoring and ongoing authorization processes currently in effect." from Appendix F, Section F.4, paragraph 2.	F-6
06-05-2014	Substantive	Added "NIST Special Publication 800-137 provides additional guidance for Information Security Continuous Monitoring Programs." to Appendix F, Section F.4, footnote 71.	F-6

DATE	TYPE	CHANGE	PAGE
06-05-2014	Substantive	Deleted "Unless otherwise handled by continuous monitoring and ongoing authorization, event-driven reauthorizations can occur when there is a significant change to an information system or its environment of operation." from Appendix F, Section F.4, paragraph 4.	F-7
06-05-2014	Substantive	Added "When an information system is under ongoing authorization, the system may be authorized for ongoing operation on a *time-driven* or *event-driven* basis, leveraging the security-related information generated by the continuous monitoring program. The system is reviewed and authorized for ongoing operation on a time-driven basis in accordance with the authorization frequency determined as part of the continuous monitoring strategy. The system is reviewed and authorized for ongoing operation on an event-driven basis when pre-defined (trigger) events occur or at the discretion of the authorizing official. Whether the authorization for ongoing operation is time-driven or event-driven, the authorizing official acknowledges ongoing acceptance of identified risks. The organization determines the level of formality required for such acknowledgement by the authorizing official." to Appendix F, Section F.4, paragraph 3.	F-7
06-05-2014	Editorial	Added new Section F.5, Reauthorization, to Appendix F.	F-7
06-05-2014	Substantive	Added "If a formal reauthorization action is required, organizations maximize the use of security and risk-related information produced as part of the continuous monitoring processes currently in effect." to Appendix F, new Section F.5, paragraph 1.	F-7
06-05-2014	Editorial	Changed "Reauthorization actions" to "Formal reauthorization actions" in Appendix F, new Section F.5, paragraph 1.	F-7
06-05-2014	Substantive	Added "(if one is specified)" to Appendix F, new Section F.5, paragraph 1.	F-7
06-05-2014	Substantive	Added "If the information system is under ongoing authorization (i.e., a continuous monitoring program is in place that monitors all implemented common, hybrid, and system-specific controls with the frequency specified in the continuous monitoring strategy), time-driven reauthorizations may not be necessary. However, if the continuous monitoring program is not yet comprehensive enough to fully support ongoing authorization, a maximum authorization period can be specified by the authorizing official." to Appendix F, new Section F.5, paragraph 1.	F-7
06-05-2014	Substantive	Added "For security control assessments associated with reauthorization, organizations leverage security-related information generated by the existing continuous monitoring program and fill in any gaps with manual or procedural assessments. Organizations may also supplement automatically-generated information with manually/procedurally-generated assessment information in situations where greater assurance is needed." to Appendix F, new Section F.5, paragraph 2.	F-7
06-05-2014	Substantive	Deleted "For example, if the maximum authorization period for an information system is three years, then an organization establishes a continuous monitoring strategy for assessing a subset of the security controls employed within and inherited by the system during the authorization period. This strategy allows all security controls designated in the respective security plans to be assessed at least one time by the end of the three-year period. This also includes any common controls deployed external to organizational information systems." from Appendix F, new Section F.5, paragraph 2.	F-7
06-05-2014	Substantive	Deleted "thus supporting the concept of ongoing authorization" from Appendix F, new Section F.5, paragraph 2.	F-7

DATE	TYPE	CHANGE	PAGE
06-05-2014	Editorial	Moved "In the event that there is a change in authorizing officials, the new authorizing official reviews the current authorization decision document, authorization package, and any updated documents created as a result of the ongoing monitoring activities. If the new authorizing official is willing to accept the currently documented risk, then the official signs a new authorization decision document, thus formally transferring responsibility and accountability for the information system or the common controls inherited by organizational information systems and explicitly accepting the risk to organizational operations and assets, individuals, other organizations, and the Nation. If the new authorizing official is not willing to accept the previous authorization results (including identified level of risk), a *reauthorization* action may need to be initiated or the new authorizing official may instead establish new terms and conditions for continuing the original authorization, but not extend the original authorization termination date. In all situations where there is a decision to reauthorize an information system or the common controls inherited by organizational information systems, the maximum reuse of authorization information is strongly encouraged to minimize the time and expense associated with the reauthorization effort." from Appendix F, Section F.4, paragraph 5 to new Section F.5, paragraph 3.	F-7
06-05-2014	Editorial	Added new Section F.6, Event-Driven Triggers, to Appendix F.	F-8
06-05-2014	Substantive	Added "Organizations may define event-driven *triggers* (i.e., indicators and/or prompts that cause a pre-defined organizational reaction) for both ongoing authorization and reauthorization. Event-driven triggers include, but are not limited to: (i) new threat/vulnerability/impact information; (ii) an increased number of findings, weaknesses, and/or deficiencies from the continuous monitoring program; (iii) new missions/business requirements; (iv) a change in the Authorizing Official; (v) a significant change in risk assessment findings; (vi) significant changes to the information system, common controls, or the environment of operation; or (vii) organizational thresholds being exceeded." to Appendix F, new Section F.6.	F-8
06-05-2014	Editorial	Changed "F.5" to "F.7" in Appendix F.	F-8
06-05-2014	Editorial	Changed "F.6" to "F.8" in Appendix F.	F-9
06-05-2014	Substantive	Deleted "Continuous monitoring is a proven technique to address the security impacts on an information system resulting from changes to the hardware, software, firmware, or operational environment." from Appendix G, paragraph 1.	G-1
06-05-2014	Substantive	Added "The following sections provide a general overview of some fundamental concepts associated with continuous monitoring. NIST Special Publication 800-137 provides additional guidance on the development and implementation of information security continuous monitoring programs." to Appendix G, paragraph 1.	G-1
06-05-2014	Substantive	Deleted "including the potential need to change or supplement the control set, taking into account any proposed/actual changes to the information system or its environment of operation" from Appendix G, Section G.1, paragraph 1.	G-1
06-05-2014	Editorial	Changed "will require" to "requires" in Appendix G, Section G.1, paragraph 3.	G-2
06-05-2014	Substantive	Changed "Configuration management and control processes for organizational information systems" to "Defining a continuous monitoring strategy based on risk tolerance that maintains clear visibility into assets, awareness of vulnerabilities, up-to-date threat information, and mission/business impacts" in Appendix G, Section G.1, paragraph 4.	G-2
06-05-2014	Substantive	Changed "Security impact analyses on proposed or actual changes to organizational information systems and environments of operation" to "Establishing and implementing a continuous monitoring program that includes monitoring all implemented controls at the organization-defined frequency" in Appendix G, Section G.1, paragraph 4.	G-2
06-05-2014	Editorial	Moved footnote 84 marking to first sentence in Appendix G, Section G.1, paragraph 4; deleted ")" from footnote 84.	G-2

DATE	TYPE	CHANGE	PAGE
06-05-2014	Editorial	Moved footnote 85 marking from third bullet to second bullet in Appendix G, Section G.1, paragraph 4.	G-2
06-05-2014	Substantive	Changed "Assessment of selected security controls (including system-specific, hybrid, and common controls) based on the organization-defined continuous monitoring strategy" to "Analyzing and reporting findings to appropriate organizational officials" in Appendix G, Section G.1, paragraph 4.	G-2
06-05-2014	Editorial	Moved footnote 86 marking from fourth bullet to third bullet in Appendix G, Section G.1, paragraph 4.	G-2
06-05-2014	Substantive	Changed "Security status reporting to appropriate organizational officials" to "Responding to findings with mitigation, acceptance, transference/sharing, or avoidance/rejection" in Appendix G, Section G.1, paragraph 4.	G-2
06-05-2014	Substantive	Changed "Active involvement by authorizing officials in the ongoing management of information system-related security risks" to "Reviewing and updating the continuous monitoring strategy and program to increase visibility into assets and awareness of vulnerabilities" in Appendix G, Section G.1, paragraph 4.	G-2
06-05-2014	Substantive	Deleted "With regard to configuration management and control, it is important to document the proposed or actual changes to the information system and its environment of operation and to subsequently determine the impact of those proposed or actual changes on the overall security state of the system. Information systems and the environments in which those systems operate are typically in a constant state of change (e.g., upgrading hardware, software, or firmware; redefining the missions and business processes of the organization; discovering new threats). Documenting information system changes as part of routine SDLC processes and assessing the potential impact those changes may have on the security state of the system is an essential aspect of continuous monitoring, maintaining the current authorization, and supporting a decision for reauthorization when appropriate." from Appendix G, Section G.1, paragraph 5.	G-2
06-05-2014	Substantive	Added "Continuous monitoring is a tactic in a larger strategy of organization-wide risk management. Organizations increase situational awareness through enhanced monitoring capabilities and subsequently increase insight into and control of the processes used to manage organizational security." to Appendix G, Section G.1, paragraph 5.	G-2
06-05-2014	Substantive	Changed "Selection of Security Controls for Monitoring" to "Frequency of Security Control Monitoring" in Appendix G, Section G.2, Title.	G-2
06-05-2014	Substantive	Deleted "selecting which security controls to monitor and for" from Appendix G, Section G.2, paragraph 1.	G-2
06-05-2014	Editorial	Changed "such" to "security control" in Appendix G, Section G.2, paragraph 1.	G-2
06-05-2014	Editorial	Changed "are" to "is" in Appendix G, Section G.2, paragraph 1.	G-2
06-05-2014	Editorial	Changed "reflect" to "reflects" in Appendix G, Section G.2, paragraph 1.	G-2
06-05-2014	Substantive	Changed "selection" to "frequency" in Appendix G, Section G.2, paragraph 1, two instances.	G-2
06-05-2014	Substantive	Changed "controls to be monitored and the frequency of the monitoring process" to "control monitoring" in Appendix G, Section G.2, paragraph 1.	G-2
06-05-2014	Substantive	Deleted "Priority for security control monitoring is given to the controls that have the greatest volatility and the controls that have been identified in the organization's plan of action and milestones." from Appendix G, Section G.2, paragraph 2.	G-3
06-05-2014	Substantive	Added "While a comprehensive discussion of considerations for determining monitoring frequencies is provided in NIST Special Publication 800-137, it is important to note that security controls that have the greatest volatility and the controls that have been identified in the organization's plan of action and milestones are typically monitored more frequently." to Appendix G, Section G.2, paragraph 2.	G-3

DATE	TYPE	CHANGE	PAGE
06-05-2014	Editorial	Deleted ", therefore," from Appendix G, Section G.2, paragraph 2.	G-3
06-05-2014	Substantive	Added "and therefore, require more frequent monitoring" to Appendix G, Section G.2, paragraph 2.	G-3
06-05-2014	Substantive	Added "Such controls may also require more frequent monitoring." to Appendix G, Section G.2, paragraph 2.	G-3
06-05-2014	Substantive	Deleted "Organizations also consider specific threat information including known attack vectors (i.e., specific vulnerabilities exploited by threat sources) when selecting the set of security controls to monitor and the frequency of such monitoring." from Appendix G, Section G.2, paragraph 2.	G-3

INTRODUCTION

THE NEED FOR INFORMATION SECURITY AND MANAGING RISK

Organizations[4] depend on information technology and the information systems[5] that are developed from that technology to successfully carry out their missions and business functions. Information systems can include as constituent components, a range of diverse computing platforms from high-end supercomputers to personal digital assistants and cellular telephones. Information systems can also include very specialized systems and devices (e.g., telecommunications systems, industrial/process control systems, testing and calibration devices, weapons systems, command and control systems, and environmental control systems). Federal information and information systems[6] are subject to serious threats that can have adverse impacts on organizational operations (including mission, functions, image, and reputation), organizational assets, individuals, other organizations, and the Nation[7] by compromising the confidentiality, integrity, or availability of information being processed, stored, or transmitted by those systems. Threats to information and information systems include environmental disruptions, human or machine errors, and purposeful attacks. Cyber attacks on information systems today are often aggressive, disciplined, well-organized, well-funded, and in a growing number of documented cases, very sophisticated. Successful attacks on public and private sector information systems can result in serious or grave damage to the national and economic security interests of the United States. Given the significant and growing danger of these threats, it is imperative that leaders at all levels of an organization understand their responsibilities for achieving adequate information security and for managing information system-related security risks.[8]

1.1 BACKGROUND

NIST in partnership with the Department of Defense (DoD), the Office of the Director of National Intelligence (ODNI), and the Committee on National Security Systems (CNSS), has developed a common information security framework for the federal government and its contractors. The intent of this common framework is to improve information security, strengthen risk management processes, and encourage reciprocity among federal agencies. This publication, developed by the Joint Task Force Transformation Initiative Working Group, transforms the traditional Certification and Accreditation (C&A) process into the six-step Risk Management Framework (RMF). The revised process emphasizes: (i) building information security capabilities into federal information systems through the application of state-of-the-practice management, operational, and technical security controls; (ii) maintaining awareness of the security state of information systems on an ongoing basis though enhanced monitoring processes; and (iii)

---

[4] The term *organization* is used in this publication to describe an entity of any size, complexity, or positioning within an organizational structure (e.g., a federal agency or, as appropriate, any of its operational elements).

[5] An *information system* is a discrete set of information resources organized for the collection, processing, maintenance, use, sharing, dissemination, or disposition of information.

[6] A *federal information system* is an information system used or operated by an executive agency, by a contractor of an executive agency, or by another organization on behalf of an executive agency.

[7] Adverse impacts to the Nation include, for example, compromises to information systems that support critical infrastructure applications or are paramount to government continuity of operations as defined by the Department of Homeland Security.

[8] Risk is a measure of the extent to which an entity is threatened by a potential circumstance or event, and a function of: (i) the adverse impacts that would arise if the circumstance or event occurs; and (ii) the likelihood of occurrence.

providing essential information to senior leaders to facilitate decisions regarding the acceptance of risk to organizational operations and assets, individuals, other organizations, and the Nation arising from the operation and use of information systems.

The RMF has the following characteristics:

- Promotes the concept of near real-time risk management and ongoing information system authorization through the implementation of robust continuous monitoring processes;

- Encourages the use of automation to provide senior leaders the necessary information to make cost-effective, risk-based decisions with regard to the organizational information systems supporting their core missions and business functions;

- Integrates information security into the enterprise architecture and system development life cycle;

- Provides emphasis on the selection, implementation, assessment, and monitoring of security controls, and the authorization of information systems;

- Links risk management processes at the information system level to risk management processes at the organization level through a risk executive (function); and

- Establishes responsibility and accountability for security controls deployed within organizational information systems and inherited by those systems (i.e., common controls).

The risk management process described in this publication changes the traditional focus of C&A as a static, procedural activity to a more dynamic approach that provides the capability to more effectively manage information system-related security risks in highly diverse environments of complex and sophisticated cyber threats, ever-increasing system vulnerabilities, and rapidly changing missions.

1.2 PURPOSE AND APPLICABILITY

The purpose of this publication is to provide guidelines for applying the Risk Management Framework to federal information systems to include conducting the activities of security categorization,[9] security control selection and implementation, security control assessment, information system authorization,[10] and security control monitoring. The guidelines have been developed:

- To ensure that managing information system-related security risks is consistent with the organization's mission/business objectives and overall risk strategy established by the senior leadership through the risk executive (function);

- To ensure that information security requirements, including necessary security controls, are integrated into the organization's enterprise architecture and system development life cycle processes;

---

[9] FIPS 199 provides security categorization guidance for nonnational security systems. CNSS Instruction 1253 provides similar guidance for national security systems.

[10] Security *authorization* is the official management decision given by a senior organizational official to authorize operation of an information system and to explicitly accept the risk to organizational operations and assets, individuals, other organizations, and the Nation based on the implementation of an agreed-upon set of security controls.

- To support consistent, well-informed, and ongoing security authorization decisions (through continuous monitoring), transparency of security and risk management-related information, and reciprocity;[11] and

- To achieve more secure information and information systems within the federal government through the implementation of appropriate risk mitigation strategies.

This publication satisfies the requirements of the Federal Information Security Management Act (FISMA) and meets or exceeds the information security requirements established for executive agencies[12] by the Office of Management and Budget (OMB) in Circular A-130, Appendix III, *Security of Federal Automated Information Resources.* The guidelines in this publication are applicable to all federal information systems other than those systems designated as national security systems as defined in 44 U.S.C., Section 3542. The guidelines have been broadly developed from a technical perspective to complement similar guidelines for national security systems and may be used for such systems with the approval of appropriate federal officials exercising policy authority over such systems. State, local, and tribal governments, as well as private sector organizations are encouraged to consider using these guidelines, as appropriate.[13]

1.3 TARGET AUDIENCE

This publication serves individuals associated with the design, development, implementation, operation, maintenance, and disposition of federal information systems including:

- Individuals with mission/business ownership responsibilities or fiduciary responsibilities (e.g., heads of federal agencies, chief executive officers, chief financial officers);

- Individuals with information system development and integration responsibilities (e.g., program managers, information technology product developers, information system developers, information systems integrators, enterprise architects, information security architects);

- Individuals with information system and/or security management/oversight responsibilities (e.g., senior leaders, risk executives, authorizing officials, chief information officers, senior information security officers[14]);

---

[11] *Reciprocity* is the mutual agreement among participating organizations to accept each other's security assessments in order to reuse information system resources and/or to accept each other's assessed security posture in order to share information. Reciprocity is best achieved by promoting the concept of transparency (i.e., making sufficient evidence regarding the security state of an information system available, so that an authorizing official from another organization can use that evidence to make credible, risk-based decisions regarding the operation and use of that system or the information it processes, stores, or transmits).

[12] An *executive agency* is: (i) an executive department specified in 5 U.S.C., Section 101; (ii) a military department specified in 5 U.S.C., Section 102; (iii) an independent establishment as defined in 5 U.S.C., Section 104(1); and (iv) a wholly owned government corporation fully subject to the provisions of 31 U.S.C., Chapter 91. In this publication, the term executive agency is synonymous with the term *federal agency.*

[13] In accordance with the provisions of FISMA and OMB policy, whenever the interconnection of federal information systems to information systems operated by state/local/tribal governments, contractors, or grantees involves the processing, storage, or transmission of federal information, the information security standards and guidelines described in this publication apply. Specific information security requirements and the terms and conditions of the system interconnections, are expressed in the Memorandums of Understanding and Interconnection Security Agreements established by participating organizations.

[14] At the *agency* level, this position is known as the Senior Agency Information Security Officer. Organizations also refer to this position as the *Chief Information Security Officer.*

- Individuals with information system and security control assessment and monitoring responsibilities (e.g., system evaluators, assessors/assessment teams, independent verification and validation assessors, auditors, or information system owners); and

- Individuals with information security implementation and operational responsibilities (e.g., information system owners, common control providers, information owners/stewards, mission/business owners, information security architects, information system security engineers/officers).

1.4 ORGANIZATION OF THIS SPECIAL PUBLICATION

The remainder of this special publication is organized as follows:

- **Chapter Two** describes the fundamental concepts associated with managing information system-related security risks including: (i) an organization-wide view of risk management and the application of the Risk Management Framework; (ii) the integration of information security requirements into the system development life cycle; (iii) the establishment of information system boundaries; and (iv) the allocation of security controls to organizational information systems as system-specific, hybrid, or common controls.

- **Chapter Three** describes the tasks required to apply the Risk Management Framework to information systems including: (i) the categorization of information and information systems; (ii) the selection of security controls; (iii) the implementation of security controls; (iv) the assessment of security control effectiveness; (v) the authorization of the information system; and (vi) the ongoing monitoring of security controls and the security state of the information system.

- **Supporting appendices** provide additional information regarding the application of the Risk Management Framework to information systems including: (i) references; (ii) glossary; (iii) acronyms; (iv) roles and responsibilities; (v) summary of Risk Management Framework tasks; (vi) security authorization of information systems; (vii) monitoring the security state of information systems; (viii) operational scenarios; and (ix) security controls in external environments.

CHAPTER TWO

THE FUNDAMENTALS

MANAGING INFORMATION SYSTEM-RELATED SECURITY RISKS

This chapter describes the basic concepts associated with managing information system-related security risks. These concepts include: (i) incorporating risk management principles and best practices into organization-wide strategic planning considerations, core missions and business processes, and supporting organizational information systems; (ii) integrating information security requirements into system development life cycle processes; (iii) establishing practical and meaningful boundaries for organizational information systems; and (iv) allocating security controls to organizational information systems as system-specific, hybrid, or common controls.

2.1 INTEGRATED ORGANIZATION-WIDE RISK MANAGEMENT

Managing information system-related security risks is a complex, multifaceted undertaking that requires the involvement of the entire organization—from senior leaders providing the strategic vision and top-level goals and objectives for the organization, to mid-level leaders planning and managing projects, to individuals on the front lines developing, implementing, and operating the systems supporting the organization's core missions and business processes. Risk management can be viewed as a holistic activity that is fully integrated into every aspect of the organization. Figure 2-1 illustrates a three-tiered approach to risk management that addresses risk-related concerns at: (i) the *organization* level; (ii) the *mission and business process* level; and (iii) the *information system* level.[15]

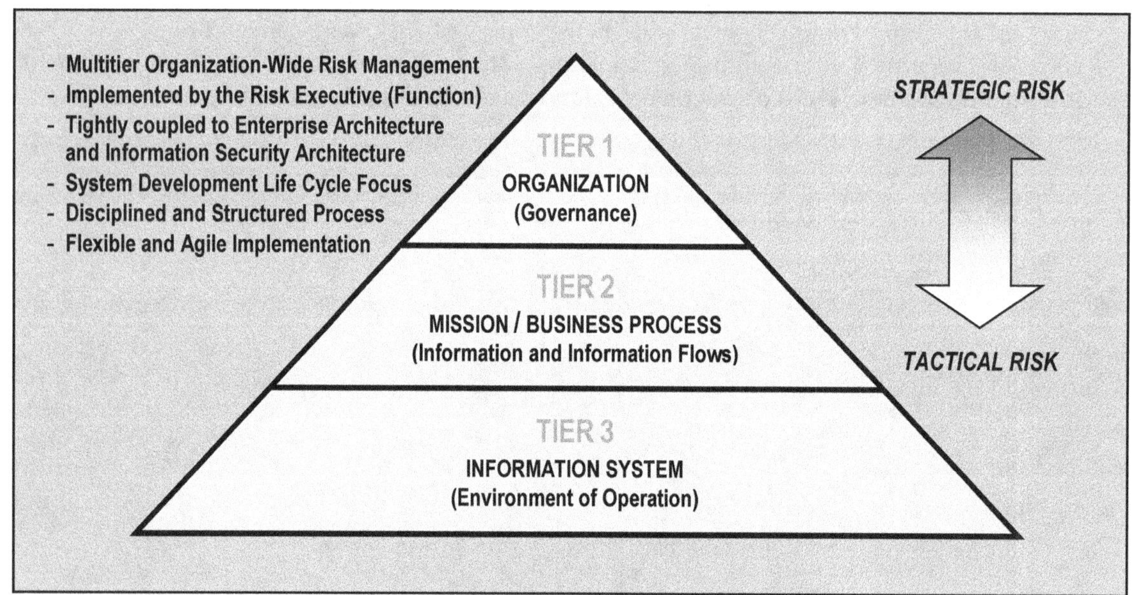

FIGURE 2-1: TIERED RISK MANAGEMENT APPROACH

---

[15] NIST Special Publication 800-39, *Integrated Enterprise-Wide Risk Management: Organization, Mission, and Information System View* (projected for publication in 2010), will provide guidance on the holistic approach to risk management.

Tier 1 addresses risk from an organizational perspective with the development of a comprehensive governance structure and organization-wide risk management strategy that includes: (i) the techniques and methodologies the organization plans to employ to assess information system-related security risks and other types of risk of concern to the organization;[16] (ii) the methods and procedures the organization plans to use to evaluate the significance of the risks identified during the risk assessment; (iii) the types and extent of risk mitigation measures the organization plans to employ to address identified risks; (iv) the level of risk the organization plans to accept (i.e., risk tolerance); (v) how the organization plans to monitor risk on an ongoing basis given the inevitable changes to organizational information systems and their environments of operation; and (vi) the degree and type of oversight the organization plans to use to ensure that the risk management strategy is being effectively carried out. As part of the overall governance structure established by the organization, the risk management strategy is propagated to organizational officials and contractors with programmatic, planning, developmental, acquisition, operational, and oversight responsibilities, including for example: (i) authorizing officials; (ii) chief information officers; (iii) senior information security officers; (iv) enterprise/information security architects; (v) information system owners/program managers; (vi) information owners/stewards; (vii) information system security officers; (viii) information system security engineers; (ix) information system developers and integrators; (x) system administrators; (xi) contracting officers; and (xii) users.

Tier 2 addresses risk from a _mission_ and _business process_ perspective and is guided by the risk decisions at **Tier 1**. **Tier 2** activities are closely associated with enterprise architecture[17] and include: (i) defining the core missions and business processes for the organization (including any derivative or related missions and business processes carried out by subordinate organizations); (ii) prioritizing missions and business processes with respect to the goals and objectives of the organization; (iii) defining the types of information that the organization needs to successfully execute the stated missions and business processes and the information flows both internal and external to the organization; (iv) developing an organization-wide information protection strategy and incorporating high-level information security requirements[18] into the core missions and business processes; and (v) specifying the degree of autonomy for subordinate organizations (i.e., organizations within the parent organization) that the parent organization permits for assessing, evaluating, mitigating, accepting, and monitoring risk.

Because subordinate organizations responsible for carrying out derivative or related missions and business processes may have already invested in their own methods of assessing, evaluating, mitigating, accepting and monitoring risk, parent organizations may allow a greater degree of autonomy within parts of the organization or across the entire organization in order to minimize costs. When a diversity of risk assessment methods is allowed, organizations may choose to employ when feasible, some means of translation and/or synthesis of the risk-related information to ensure that the output of the different risk assessment activities can be correlated in a meaningful manner.

---

[16] Types of _risk_ include, for example: (i) program/acquisition risk (cost, schedule, performance); (ii) compliance and regulatory risk; (iii) financial risk; (iv) legal risk; (v) operational (mission/business) risk; (vi) political risk; (vii) project risk; (viii) reputational risk; (ix) safety risk; (x) strategic planning risk; and (xi) supply chain risk.

[17] Federal Enterprise Architecture Reference Models and Segment and Solution Architectures are defined in the OMB Federal Enterprise Architecture (FEA) Program, _FEA Consolidated Reference Model Document,_ Version 2.3, October 2003 and OMB _Federal Segment Architecture Methodology (FSAM),_ January 2009, respectively.

[18] Information security requirements can be obtained from a variety of sources (e.g., legislation, policies, directives, regulations, standards, and organizational mission/business/operational requirements). Organization-level security requirements are documented in the information security program plan or equivalent document.

Tier 3 addresses risk from an *information system* perspective and is guided by the risk decisions at **Tiers 1** and **2**. Risk decisions at **Tiers 1** and **2** impact the ultimate selection and deployment of needed safeguards and countermeasures (i.e., security controls) at the information system level. Information security requirements are satisfied by the selection of appropriate management, operational, and technical security controls from NIST Special Publication 800-53.[19] The security controls are subsequently allocated to the various components of the information system as system-specific, hybrid, or common controls in accordance with the information security architecture developed by the organization.[20] Security controls are typically *traceable* to the security requirements established by the organization to ensure that the requirements are fully addressed during design, development, and implementation of the information system. Security controls can be provided by the organization or by an external provider. Relationships with external providers are established in a variety of ways, for example, through joint ventures, business partnerships, outsourcing arrangements (i.e., through contracts, interagency agreements, lines of business arrangements), licensing agreements, and/or supply chain arrangements.[21]

Risk management tasks begin early in the system development life cycle and are important in shaping the security capabilities of the information system. If these tasks are not adequately performed during the initiation, development, and acquisition phases of the system development life cycle, the tasks will, by necessity, be undertaken later in the life cycle and be more costly to implement. In either situation, all tasks are completed prior to placing the information system into operation or continuing its operation to ensure that: (i) information system-related security risks are being adequately addressed on an ongoing basis; and (ii) the authorizing official explicitly understands and accepts the risk to organizational operations and assets, individuals, other organizations, and the Nation based on the implementation of a defined set of security controls and the current security state of the information system.

The Risk Management Framework (RMF), illustrated in Figure 2-2, provides a disciplined and structured process that integrates information security and risk management activities into the system development life cycle. The RMF operates primarily at **Tier 3** in the risk management hierarchy but can also have interactions at **Tiers 1** and **2** (e.g., providing feedback from ongoing authorization decisions to the risk executive [function], dissemination of updated threat and risk information to authorizing officials and information system owners). The RMF steps include:

- *Categorize* the information system and the information processed, stored, and transmitted by that system based on an impact analysis.[22]

- *Select* an initial set of baseline security controls for the information system based on the security categorization; tailoring and supplementing the security control baseline as needed based on an organizational assessment of risk and local conditions.[23]

---

[19] The RMF categorization step, including consideration of legislation, policies, directives, regulations, standards, and organizational mission/business/operational requirements, facilitates the identification of security requirements.

[20] The allocation of security controls can take place at all three tiers in the risk management hierarchy. For example, security controls that are identified as common controls may be allocated at the organization, mission/business process, or information system level. See Section 2.4 for additional information on security control allocation.

[21] Appendix I provides additional guidance regarding external service providers and the provision of security controls in external environments.

[22] FIPS 199 provides security categorization guidance for nonnational security systems. CNSS Instruction 1253 provides similar guidance for national security systems.

[23] NIST Special Publication 800-53 provides security control selection guidance for nonnational security systems. CNSS Instruction 1253 provides similar guidance for national security systems.

- ***Implement*** the security controls and describe how the controls are employed within the information system and its environment of operation.

- ***Assess*** the security controls using appropriate assessment procedures to determine the extent to which the controls are implemented correctly, operating as intended, and producing the desired outcome with respect to meeting the security requirements for the system.

- ***Authorize*** information system operation based on a determination of the risk to organizational operations and assets, individuals, other organizations, and the Nation resulting from the operation of the information system and the decision that this risk is acceptable.

- ***Monitor*** the security controls in the information system on an ongoing basis including assessing control effectiveness, documenting changes to the system or its environment of operation, conducting security impact analyses of the associated changes, and reporting the security state of the system to designated organizational officials.

Chapter Three provides a detailed description of each of the specific tasks necessary to carry out the six steps in the RMF.

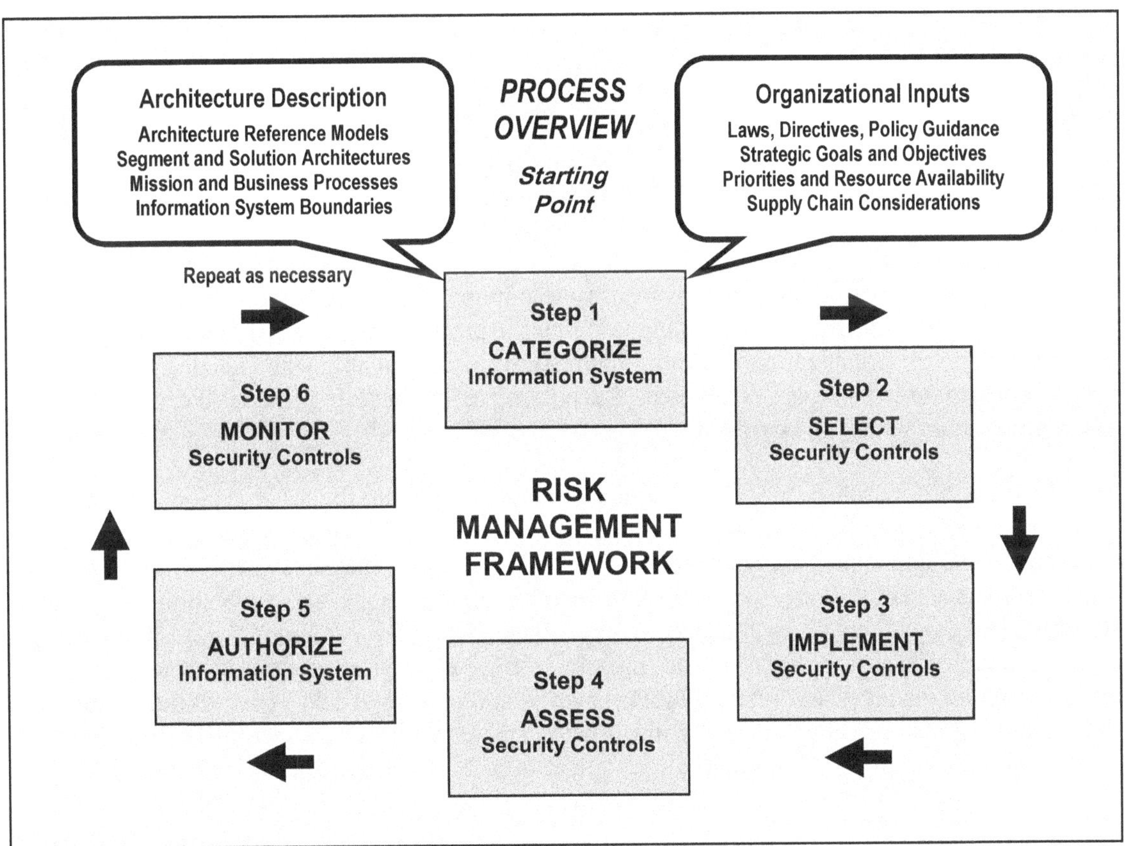

FIGURE 2-2: RISK MANAGEMENT FRAMEWORK

In summary, there is a significant degree of flexibility in how organizations employ the risk management processes described above. While it is convenient to portray the risk management approach in Figure 2-1 as hierarchical, the reality of project and organization dynamics can be much more complex. The organizational management style may be at one or more points on the continuum from top-down command to consensus among peers. For risk management to succeed at all levels of the organization, the organization must have a consistent and effective approach to risk management that is applied to all risk management processes and procedures. Organizational officials identify the resources necessary to complete the risk management tasks described in this publication and ensure that those resources are made available to appropriate personnel. Resource allocation includes both funding to carry out the risk management tasks and assigning qualified personnel needed to accomplish the tasks.[24]

2.2 SYSTEM DEVELOPMENT LIFE CYCLE

All federal information systems, including operational systems, systems under development, and systems undergoing modification or upgrade, are in some phase of a system development life cycle.[25] Requirements definition is a critical part of any system development process and begins very early in the life cycle, typically in the *initiation* phase.[26] Security requirements are a subset of the overall functional and nonfunctional (e.g., quality, assurance) requirements levied on an information system and are incorporated into the system development life cycle simultaneously with the functional and nonfunctional requirements. Without the early integration of security requirements, significant expense may be incurred by the organization later in the life cycle to address security considerations that could have been included in the initial design. When security requirements are considered as an integral subset of other information system requirements, the resulting system has fewer weaknesses and deficiencies, and therefore, fewer vulnerabilities that can be exploited in the future.

Early integration of information security requirements into the system development life cycle is the most cost-effective and efficient method for an organization to ensure that its protection strategy is implemented. It also ensures that information security processes are not isolated from the other routine management processes employed by the organization to develop, implement, operate, and maintain information systems supporting ongoing missions and business functions. In addition to incorporating information security requirements into the system development life cycle, security requirements are also integrated into the program, planning, and budgeting activities within the organization to ensure that resources are available when needed and program/project milestones are completed. The enterprise architecture provides a central record of this integration within an organization.

Ensuring that information security requirements are integrated into the organization's system development life cycle processes regardless of the type of life cycle processes employed, helps facilitate development and implementation of more resilient information systems to reduce risk to organizational operations and assets, individuals, other organizations, and the Nation. This can be accomplished using the well-established concept of *integrated project teams*.[27] A responsible organizational official (e.g., agency head, mission or business owner, integrated project team leader, program manager, information system owner, authorizing official) ensures that security professionals are an integral part of any information system development activities from the initial definition of information security requirements at **Tier 1** and **Tier 2** to the selection of

---

[24] Resource requirements include funding for training organizational personnel to ensure that they can effectively carry out their assigned responsibilities.

[25] There are typically five phases in a generic system development life cycle including: (i) *initiation*; (ii) *development/ acquisition*; (iii) *implementation*; (iv) *operation/maintenance*; and (v) *disposal*.

[26] Organizations may employ a variety of system development life cycle processes including, for example, waterfall, spiral, or agile development.

[27] Integrated project teams are multidisciplinary entities consisting of a number of individuals with a range of skills and roles to help facilitate the development of information systems that meet the requirements of the organization.

security controls at **Tier 3**. Such consideration is used to foster close cooperation among personnel responsible for the design, development, implementation, operation, maintenance, and disposition of information systems and the information security professionals advising the senior leadership on appropriate security controls needed to adequately mitigate risk and protect critical missions and business functions.

Finally, organizations maximize the use of security-relevant information (e.g., assessment results, information system documentation, and other artifacts) generated during the system development life cycle to satisfy requirements for similar information needed for information security-related purposes. Similar security-relevant information concerning common controls, including security controls provided by external providers, is factored into the organization's risk management process. The judicious reuse of security-relevant information by organizations is an effective method to help eliminate duplication of effort, reduce documentation, promote reciprocity, and avoid unnecessary costs that may result when security activities are conducted independently of system development life cycle processes. In addition, reuse promotes greater consistency of information used in the design, development, implementation, operation, maintenance, and disposition of an information system including security-related considerations.

2.3 INFORMATION SYSTEM BOUNDARIES

One of the most challenging problems for information system owners, authorizing officials, chief information officers, senior information security officers, and information security architects is identifying appropriate boundaries for organizational information systems.[28] Well-defined boundaries establish the scope of protection for organizational information systems (i.e., what the organization agrees to protect under its direct management control or within the scope of its responsibilities) and include the people, processes, and information technologies that are part of the systems supporting the organization's missions and business processes. Information system boundaries are established in coordination with the security categorization process and before the development of security plans. Information system boundaries that are too expansive (i.e., too many system components and/or unnecessary architectural complexity) make the risk management process extremely unwieldy and complex. Boundaries that are too limited increase the number of information systems that must be separately managed and as a consequence, unnecessarily inflate the total information security costs for the organization. The following sections provide general guidelines to assist organizations in establishing appropriate system boundaries to achieve cost-effective solutions for managing information security-related risks from the operation and use of information systems.

2.3.1 Establishing Information System Boundaries

The set of information resources[29] allocated to an information system defines the boundary for that system. Organizations have significant flexibility in determining what constitutes an information system and its associated boundary. If a set of information resources is identified as an information system, the resources are generally under the same direct management control.[30] Direct management control does not necessarily imply that there is no intervening management.

---

[28] With regard to the risk management process and information security, the term *information system boundary* is synonymous with *authorization boundary*.

[29] Information resources consist of information and related resources including personnel, equipment, funds, and information technology.

[30] For information systems, direct management control involves budgetary, programmatic, or operational authority and associated *responsibility* and *accountability*.

It is also possible for multiple information systems to be considered as independent *subsystems*[31] of a more complex information system. This situation may arise in many organizations when smaller information systems are coalesced for purposes of risk management into a larger, more comprehensive system. On a larger scale, an organization may develop a *system of systems* involving multiple independent information systems (possibly distributed across a widespread geographic area) supporting a set of common missions and/or business functions.[32]

In addition to consideration of direct management control, it may also be helpful for organizations to determine if the information resources being identified as an information system:

- Support the same mission/business objectives or functions and essentially the same operating characteristics and information security requirements; and

- Reside in the same general operating environment (or in the case of a distributed information system, reside in various locations with similar operating environments).[33]

Since commonality can change over time, this determination is revisited periodically as part of a continuous monitoring process carried out by the organization (see Section 3.6). While the above considerations may be useful to organizations in determining information system boundaries for purposes of risk management, they are not viewed as limiting the organization's flexibility in establishing commonsense boundaries that promote effective information security within the available resources of the organization. Information system owners consult with authorizing officials, chief information officers, senior information security officers, information security architects, and the risk executive (function)[34] when establishing or changing system boundaries. The process of establishing information system boundaries and the associated risk management implications is an organization-wide activity that includes careful negotiation among all key participants—taking into account mission and business requirements, technical considerations with respect to information security, and programmatic costs to the organization.

Software *applications* (e.g., database applications, Web applications) hosted by an information system are included in the risk management process since application security is critical to the overall security of the system.[35] Software *applications* depend on the resources provided by the hosting information system and as such, can take advantage of (i.e., leverage) the security controls provided by the system to help provide a foundational level of protection for the hosted applications, when this type of inheritance is applicable. Additional application-level security controls are provided by the respective software applications, as needed. Organizations ensure that all security controls, including application-level controls employed in separate software applications, are managed and tracked on an ongoing basis. Application owners coordinate with information system owners to ensure that information security and risk management activities are carried out as seamlessly as possible among applications and hosting systems. This coordination includes, for example, consideration for: (i) the selection, implementation, assessment, and monitoring of security controls for hosted applications; (ii) the effects of changes to hosted applications on the overall security state of the information system and the missions and business

---

[31] A *subsystem* is a major subdivision of an information system consisting of information, information technology, and personnel that perform one or more specific functions.

[32] The National Airspace System (NAS) operated by the Federal Aviation Administration (FAA) is an example of a system of systems.

[33] Similarity of operating environments includes, for example, consideration of threat, policy, and management.

[34] The roles and responsibilities of the risk executive (function) are described in Appendix D.

[35] Software applications and information systems hosting the applications may be owned by different organizations.

processes supported by that system; and (iii) the effects of changes to the information system on hosted applications. Employing strong configuration management and control processes within software applications and the hosting information system, and reusing security control assessment results helps to provide the necessary protection for applications.

Security controls provided by the hosted software application are documented in the security plan for the hosting information system and assessed for effectiveness during the risk management process (i.e., during the initial authorization of the information system and subsequently, during the continuous monitoring process). Application-level security controls are also assessed for effectiveness if the applications are added after the hosting information system is authorized to operate. Information system owners take appropriate measures to ensure that hosted applications do not affect the security state of the hosting system and obtain the necessary information from application owners to conduct security impact analyses, when needed.

2.3.2 Boundaries for Complex Information Systems

The application of security controls within a complex information system can present significant challenges to an organization. From a centralized development, implementation, and operations perspective, the information system owner, in collaboration with the authorizing official, senior information security officer, information security architect, and information system security engineer, examines the purpose of the information system and considers the feasibility of decomposing the complex system into more manageable *subsystems*. From a distributed development, implementation, and operations perspective, the organization recognizes that multiple entities, possibly operating under different policies, may be contributing to the development, implementation, and/or operations of the subsystems that compose the complex information system. In such a scenario, the organization is responsible for ensuring that these separate subsystems can work together in both a secure and functional manner. Treating an information system as multiple subsystems, each with its own subsystem boundary, facilitates a more targeted application of security controls to achieve adequate security and a more cost-effective risk management process. Knowledge of the security properties of individual subsystems does not necessarily provide the complete knowledge of the security properties of the complex information system. The organization applies best practices in systems and security engineering and documents the decomposition of the information system in the security plan.

Information security architecture plays a key part in the security control selection and allocation process for a complex information system. This includes monitoring and controlling communications at key internal boundaries among subsystems and providing system-wide *common controls* (see Section 2.4) that meet or exceed the requirements of the constituent subsystems inheriting those system-wide common controls. One approach to security control selection and allocation is to categorize each identified subsystem (including dynamic subsystems as described in Section 2.3.3). Separately categorizing each subsystem does not change the overall categorization of the information system. Rather, it allows the subsystems to receive a separate and more targeted allocation of security controls from NIST Special Publication 800-53 instead of deploying higher-impact controls across every subsystem. Another approach is to bundle smaller subsystems into larger subsystems within the overall complex information system, categorize each of the aggregated subsystems, and allocate security controls to the subsystems, as needed. While subsystems within complex information systems may exist as complete systems, the subsystems are, in most cases, not treated as independent entities because they are typically interdependent and interconnected.

When the results of security categorizations for the identified subsystems are different, the organization carefully examines the interfaces, information flows, and security-relevant dependencies[36] among subsystems and selects security controls for the interconnection of the subsystems to eliminate or reduce potential vulnerabilities in this area. This helps to ensure that the information system is adequately protected.[37] Security controls for the interconnection of subsystems are also employed when the subsystems implement different security policies or are administered by different authorities. The extent to which the security controls are implemented correctly, operating as intended, and producing the desired outcome with respect to meeting the security requirements for the complex information system, can be determined by combining security control assessments at the subsystem level and adding system-level considerations addressing interface issues among subsystems. This approach facilitates a more targeted and cost-effective risk management process by scaling the level of effort of the assessment in accordance with the subsystem security categorization and allowing for reuse of assessment results at the information system level. Figure 2-3 illustrates the concept of decomposition for a complex information system.

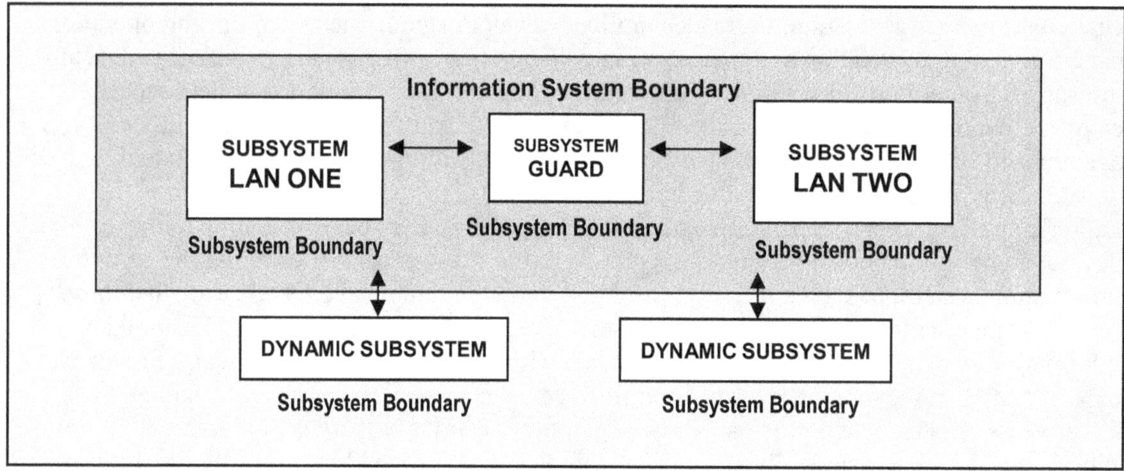

FIGURE 2-3: DECOMPOSITION OF COMPLEX INFORMATION SYSTEM

In the above example, an information system contains a system guard that monitors the flow of information between two local area networks. The information system can be partitioned into multiple subsystems: (i) local area network one; (ii) local area network two; (iii) the system guard separating the two networks; and (iv) several dynamic subsystems that become part of the system at various points in time (see Section 2.3.3). Each subsystem within the information system may be categorized individually. The security categorization of the information system as a whole is not changed by taking into consideration all of the individual subsystem categorizations. When all

---

[36] Subsystem interfaces include ports and protocols. Information flows address information transmitted between subsystems. Security-relevant dependencies refer to security functions/services (e.g., encryption, auditing), performed by one subsystem that are required by one or more of the other subsystems.

[37] The types of interfaces and couplings among subsystems may introduce inadvertent weaknesses and vulnerabilities in a complex information system. For example, if a large organizational intranet is decomposed by enterprise services into smaller subsystems (e.g., severable subsystems such as local area network segments) and subsequently categorized individually, the specific protections at the subsystem level may allow a vector of attack against the intranet by erroneously selecting and implementing security controls that are not sufficiently strong with respect to the rest of the system. To avoid this situation, organizations carefully examine the interfaces among subsystems and take appropriate actions to eliminate potential vulnerabilities in this area, thus helping to ensure that the information system is adequately protected.

subsystems within the complex information system have completed an initial security control assessment, the organization takes additional measures to ensure that: (i) security controls not included in the subsystem assessments are assessed for effectiveness; and (ii) the subsystems work together in a manner that meets the security requirements of the information system.[38]

2.3.3 Changing Technologies and the Effect on Information System Boundaries

Changes to current information technologies and computing paradigms add complications to the traditional tasks of establishing information system boundaries and protecting the missions and business processes supported by organizational information systems. In particular, net-centric architectures[39] (e.g., service-oriented architectures [SOAs], cloud computing) introduce two important concepts: (i) *dynamic subsystems*; and (ii) *external subsystems*. While the concepts of dynamic subsystems and external subsystems (described in the following sections) are not new, the pervasiveness and frequency of their invocation in net-centric architectures can present organizations with significant new challenges.

Dynamic Subsystems

For many information systems, the determination of subsystems is established at system initiation and maintained throughout the life cycle of the system. However, there are some instances, most notably in net-centric architectures, where the subsystems that compose the system may not be present at all stages of the life cycle. Some subsystems may not become part of an information system until sometime after system initiation, while other subsystems may leave the system sometime prior to system termination. Generally, this will not impact the external boundary of the information system if the dynamic subsystems are in the system design and the appropriate security controls are reflected in the security plan. But it does impact the subsystems that exist within the boundary at any given point in time.

Dynamic subsystems that become part of an organizational information system at various points in time may or may not be under the direct control of the organization. These subsystems may be provided by external providers (e.g., through contracts, interagency agreements, lines of business arrangements, licensing agreements, and/or supply chain arrangements). Regardless of whether the subsystem is or is not controlled by the organization, the expectations of its capabilities have to be considered. The dynamic inclusion or exclusion of the subsystems may or may not require reassessment of the information system as a whole. This is determined based on constraints and assumptions (e.g., functions the subsystems perform, connections to other subsystems and other information systems) imposed upon the subsystems at system design and incorporated in the security plan. So long as the subsystems conform to the identified constraints and assumptions, they can be dynamically added or removed from the information system without requiring reassessments of the entire system.

---

[38] The organization can: (i) issue a single authorization for the entire complex information system (to include bundling assessment results from individual subsystem assessments and any additional assessment results at the system level); or (ii) implement a strategy for managing the risk associated with connecting separately authorized information systems when viewed as a system of systems.

[39] A net-centric architecture is a complex system of systems comprised of subsystems and services that are part of a continuously evolving, complex community of people, devices, information, and services interconnected by a network that enhances information sharing and collaboration. A service-oriented architecture (SOA) is an example of a net-centric architecture.

As noted above, the assumptions and constraints on the dynamic subsystems are reflected in the information system design and the security plan. The determination as to whether the subsystems conform to the assumptions and constraints is addressed during the continuous monitoring phase of the risk management process. Depending upon the nature of the subsystems (including the functions, connections, and relative trust relationships established with the subsystem providers), the determination of conformance may be performed in a manual or automated manner, and may occur prior to, or during the subsystem connecting/disconnecting to the information system.

External Subsystems

Another characteristic often apparent in net-centric architectures is that some of the subsystems (or components of subsystems)[40] are outside of the direct control of the organization that owns the information system and authorizes its operation. The nature of such external subsystems can vary from organizations employing external cloud computing services to process, store, and transmit information to organizations allowing platforms under their control to host applications/services developed by some external entity.

As noted in Appendix I (Security Controls in External Environments), FISMA and OMB policy require external providers handling federal information or operating information systems on behalf of the federal government to meet the same security requirements as federal agencies. These security requirements also apply to external subsystems storing, processing, or transmitting federal information and any services provided by or associated with the subsystem. Appendix I further notes that the assurance or confidence that the risk from using external services is at an acceptable level depends on the trust that the organization places in the external service provider. In some cases, the level of trust is based on the amount of direct control the organization is able to exert on the external service provider with regard to employment of security controls necessary for the protection of the service and the evidence brought forth as to the effectiveness of those controls. In other instances, trust may be based on other factors, such as the experience the organization has with the external service provider, and the confidence (trust) the organization has in the provider taking the correct actions. There are a variety of factors that can complicate the level of trust issue in the case of net-centric architectures to include:

- The delineation between what is owned by the external entity and the organization may be somewhat blurred (e.g., organization-owned platform executing external entity-developed service/application software or firmware);

- The degree of control the organization has over the external entity providing/supporting the subsystems/services may be very limited;

- The nature and content of the subsystems may be subject to rapid change; and

- The subsystems/services may be of such critical nature that they need to be incorporated into organizational information systems very rapidly.

The consequence of the factors above is that some of the more traditional means of verifying the correct functioning of a subsystem and the effectiveness of security controls (e.g., clearly defined requirements, design analysis, testing and evaluation before deployment) may not be feasible for a net-centric subsystem/service. As a result, organizations may be left to depend upon the nature of the trust relationships with the suppliers of the net-centric subsystems/services as the basis for determining whether or not to allow/include the subsystems/services (e.g., use of GSA list of approved providers). Alternatively, organizations may allow such subsystems/services to be used

---

[40] In this context, the term subsystem includes the *services* provided by or associated with that subsystem.

only in those instances where they have constrained the nature of information or process flow such that the organization believes that any potential adverse impact is manageable. Ultimately, when the level of trust in the external provider of subsystems/services is below expectations, the organization: (i) employs compensating controls; (ii) accepts a greater degree of risk; or (iii) does not obtain the service (i.e., performs its core missions and business operations with reduced levels of functionality or possibly no functionality at all).

2.4 SECURITY CONTROL ALLOCATION

There are three types of security controls for information systems that can be employed by an organization: (i) *system-specific controls* (i.e., controls that provide a security capability for a particular information system only); (ii) *common controls* (i.e., controls that provide a security capability for multiple information systems); or (iii) *hybrid controls* (i.e., controls that have both system-specific and common characteristics).[41] The organization *allocates* security controls to an information system consistent with the organization's enterprise architecture and information security architecture.[42] This activity is carried out as an organization-wide activity involving authorizing officials, information system owners, chief information security officer, senior information security officer, enterprise architect, information security architect, information system security officers, common control providers, and risk executive (function).

As part of the information security architecture, organizations are encouraged to identify and implement security controls that can support multiple information systems efficiently and effectively as a common capability (i.e., common controls). When these controls are used to support a specific information system, they are referenced by that specific system as *inherited controls*. Common controls promote more cost-effective and consistent information security across the organization and can also simplify risk management activities. By allocating security controls to an information system as system-specific controls, hybrid controls, or common controls, the organization assigns responsibility and accountability to specific organizational entities for the overall development, implementation, assessment, authorization, and monitoring of those controls.

The organization has significant flexibility in deciding which families of security controls or specific controls from selected families in NIST Special Publication 800-53 are appropriate for the different types of allocations. Since the security control allocation process involves the assignment and provision of security capabilities derived from security controls, the organization ensures that there is effective communication among all entities either receiving or providing such capabilities. This communication includes, for example, ensuring that common control authorization results and continuous monitoring information are readily available to those organizational entities inheriting common controls, and that any changes to common controls are effectively communicated to those affected by such changes.[43]

---

[41] NIST Special Publication 800-53 provides additional guidance on security controls for information systems.

[42] *Allocation* is a term used to describe the process an organization employs: (i) to determine whether security controls are defined as system-specific, hybrid, or common; and (ii) to assign security controls to specific information system components responsible for providing a particular security capability (e.g., router, server, remote sensor).

[43] Communication regarding the security status of common (inherited) controls is essential irrespective of whether the common control provider is internal or external to the organization. Appendix I provides guidance for organizations relying on security controls in external environments including the types of contractual agreements and arrangements that are necessary to ensure appropriate security-relevant information is conveyed to the organization from external providers.

Figure 2-4 illustrates security control allocation within an organization and using the RMF to produce information for senior leaders (including authorizing officials) on the ongoing security state of organizational information systems and the missions and business processes supported by those systems.

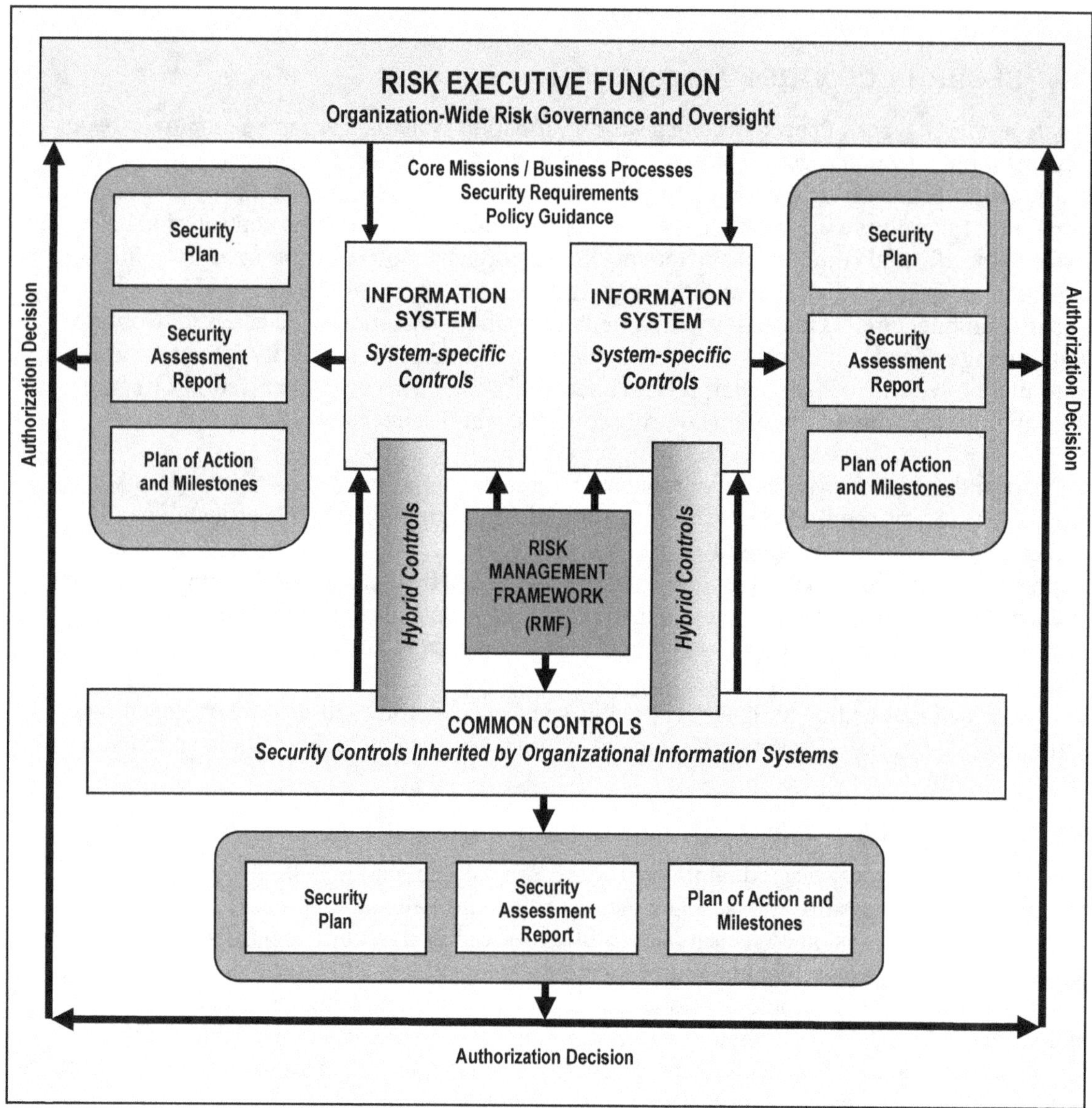

FIGURE 2-4: SECURITY CONTROL ALLOCATION

CHAPTER THREE

THE PROCESS

EXECUTING THE RISK MANAGEMENT FRAMEWORK TASKS

This chapter describes the process of applying the Risk Management Framework (RMF) to federal information systems.[44] The process includes a set of well-defined risk-related tasks that are to be carried out by selected individuals or groups within well-defined organizational roles (e.g., risk executive [function], authorizing official, authorizing official designated representative, chief information officer, senior information security officer, enterprise architect, information security architect, information owner/steward, information system owner, common control provider, information system security officer, and security control assessor).[45] Many risk management roles defined in this publication have counterpart roles defined in the routine system development life cycle processes carried out by organizations. Whenever possible and consistent with core missions/business processes, organizations align risk management roles with similar (or complementary) roles defined for the system development life cycle. RMF tasks are executed concurrently with or as part of system development life cycle processes, taking into account appropriate dependencies. This helps to ensure that organizations are effectively integrating the process of managing information system-related security risks with system development life cycle processes.

Each RMF task description includes the individual or group with the primary responsibility for carrying out the task, the supporting roles that may be called upon to assist in completing the task, the system development life cycle phase most closely associated with the task, supplemental guidance to help explain how the task is executed, and appropriate references for publications or Web sites with information related to the task.[46] To summarize the key risk management-related activities to be carried out by the organization, a milestone checkpoint is provided for each step in the RMF. The milestone checkpoints contain a series of questions for the organization to help ensure that important activities described in a particular step in the RMF have been completed prior to proceeding to the next step.

The process of implementing the RMF tasks (i.e., the order and manner in which the tasks occur and are executed, the names of primary/supporting roles, the names and format of artifacts) may vary from organization to organization. The RMF tasks can be applied at appropriate phases in the system development life cycle. While the tasks appear in sequential order, there can be many points in the risk management process that require divergence from the sequential order including the need for iterative cycles between tasks and revisiting tasks. For example, the results from security control assessments can trigger remediation actions on the part of an information system owner, which can in turn require the reassessment of selected controls. Monitoring the security

---

[44] The process for managing risk described in this publication can be tailored to meet the needs of many communities of interest within the federal government including, for example, the Civil, Defense, and Intelligence Communities. Tailoring provides flexibility in applying the risk management concepts associated with the RMF in a manner that is most suitable for the organizations and the information systems involved.

[45] Appendix D describes the roles and responsibilities of key participants involved in an organization's risk management process.

[46] A reference is included in the RMF task list if: (i) the reference is generally applicable to both national security systems and nonnational security systems; (ii) the reference for nonnational security systems has an equivalent or supporting reference for national security systems; or (iii) the reference relates to specific national security community guidance regarding the implementation of certain NIST standards or guidelines.

controls in an information system can also generate a potential cycle of tracking changes to the system and its environment of operation, conducting security impact analyses, taking remediation actions, reassessing security controls, and reporting the security status of the system. There may also be other opportunities to diverge from the sequential nature of the tasks when it is more efficient or cost-effective to do so. For example, while the security control assessment tasks are listed after the security control implementation tasks, some organizations may choose to begin the assessment of certain controls as soon as they are implemented but prior to the complete implementation of all controls described in the security plan. This may result in the organization assessing the physical and environmental protection controls within a facility prior to assessing the security controls employed in the hardware and software components of the information system (which may be implemented at a later time). Regardless of the task ordering, the last step before an information system is placed into operation is the explicit acceptance of risk by the authorizing official.

RMF steps and associated tasks can be applied to both new development and legacy information systems. For legacy systems, organizations can use RMF Steps 1 through 3 to confirm that the security categorization has been completed and is appropriate and that the requisite security controls have been selected and allocated. Applying the first three steps in the RMF to legacy systems can be viewed as a *gap analysis* to determine if the necessary and sufficient security controls (i.e., system-specific, hybrid, and common controls) have been appropriately selected and allocated. Security control weaknesses and deficiencies, if discovered, can be subsequently addressed in RMF Steps 3 through 6 similar to new development systems. If no weaknesses or deficiencies are discovered in the security controls during the gap analysis and there is a current security authorization in effect, the organization can move directly to the last step in the RMF, continuous monitoring. If a current security authorization is not in place, the organization continues with RMF Steps 4 through 6.

The security categorization process influences the level of effort expended when implementing the RMF tasks. Information systems supporting the most critical and/or sensitive operations and assets within the organization as indicated by the security categorization, demand the greatest level of attention and effort to ensure that appropriate information security and risk mitigation are achieved. Most RMF tasks can be carried out by external providers with appropriate contractual agreements or other arrangements in place (see Appendix I). A summary table of the RMF tasks is provided in Appendix E.

APPLICATION OF THE RISK MANAGEMENT FRAMEWORK

The Risk Management Framework and associated RMF tasks apply to both ***information system owners*** and ***common control providers***. In addition to supporting the authorization of information systems, the RMF tasks support the selection, development, implementation, assessment, authorization, and ongoing monitoring of common controls inherited by organizational information systems. Execution of the RMF tasks by common control providers, both internal and external to the organization, helps to ensure that the security capabilities provided by the common controls can be inherited by information system owners with a degree of assurance appropriate for their information protection needs. This approach recognizes the importance of security control effectiveness within information systems and the infrastructure supporting those systems.

Since the tasks in the RMF are described in a ***sequential*** manner, organizations may choose to deviate from that sequential structure in order to be consistent with their established management and system development life cycle processes or to achieve more cost-effective and efficient solutions with regard to the execution of the tasks. Regardless of the task ordering, the last step before an information system is placed into operation is the explicit acceptance of risk by the authorizing official. Organizations may also execute certain RMF tasks in an iterative manner or in different phases of the system development life cycle. For example, security control assessments may be carried out during system development, system implementation, and system operation/maintenance (as part of continuous monitoring).

Organizations may also choose to expend a greater ***level of effort*** on certain RMF tasks and commit fewer resources to other tasks based on the level of maturity of selected processes and activities within the organization. Since the RMF is life cycle-based, there will be a need to revisit various tasks over time depending on how the organization manages changes to the information systems and the environments in which those systems operate. Managing information security-related risks for an information system is viewed as part of a larger organization-wide risk management activity carried out by senior leaders. The RMF must simultaneously provide a disciplined and structured approach to mitigating risks from the operation and use of organizational information systems and the flexibility and agility to support the core missions and business operations of the organization in highly dynamic environments of operation.

3.1 RMF STEP 1 – CATEGORIZE INFORMATION SYSTEM

SECURITY CATEGORIZATION

TASK 1-1: Categorize the information system and document the results of the security categorization in the security plan.

Primary Responsibility: Information System Owner; Information Owner/Steward.

Supporting Roles: Risk Executive (Function); Authorizing Official or Designated Representative; Chief Information Officer; Senior Information Security Officer; Information System Security Officer.

System Development Life Cycle Phase: Initiation (concept/requirements definition).

Supplemental Guidance: The security categorization process is carried out by the information system owner and information owner/steward in cooperation and collaboration with appropriate organizational officials (i.e., senior leaders with mission/business function and/or risk management responsibilities). The security categorization process is conducted as an organization-wide activity taking into consideration the enterprise architecture and the information security architecture. This helps to ensure that individual information systems are categorized based on the mission and business objectives of the organization. The information system owner and information owner/steward consider results from the initial risk assessment as a part of the security categorization decision. The security categorization decision is consistent with the organization's *risk management strategy* to identify potential impact to mission/business functions resulting from the loss of confidentiality, integrity, and/or availability. The risk management strategy provides guidance and relevant information to authorizing officials (e.g., risk assessment methodologies employed by the organization, evaluation of risks determined, risk mitigation approaches, organizational risk tolerance, approaches for monitoring risk over time, known existing aggregated risks from current information systems, and other sources of risk).

The results of the security categorization process influence the selection of appropriate security controls for the information system and also, where applicable, the minimum assurance requirements for that system. Security categorization determinations consider potential adverse impacts to organizational operations, organizational assets, individuals, other organizations, and the Nation. The organization may consider decomposing the information system into multiple subsystems to more efficiently and effectively allocate security controls to the system. One approach is to categorize each identified subsystem (including dynamic subsystems). Separately categorizing each subsystem does not change the overall categorization of the information system. Rather, it allows the constituent subsystems to receive a separate allocation of security controls from NIST Special Publication 800-53 instead of deploying higher-impact controls across every subsystem. Another approach is to bundle smaller subsystems into larger subsystems within the information system, categorize each of the aggregated subsystems, and allocate security controls to the subsystems, as appropriate. Security categorization information is documented in the system identification section of the security plan or included as an attachment to the plan.

References: FIPS Publication 199; NIST Special Publications 800-30, 800-39, 800-59, 800-60; CNSS Instruction 1253.

INFORMATION SYSTEM DESCRIPTION

TASK 1-2: Describe the information system (including system boundary) and document the description in the security plan.

Primary Responsibility: Information System Owner.

Supporting Roles: Authorizing Official or Designated Representative; Senior Information Security Officer; Information Owner/Steward; Information System Security Officer.

System Development Life Cycle Phase: Initiation (concept/requirements definition).

Supplemental Guidance: Descriptive information about the information system is documented in the *system identification* section of the security plan, included in attachments to the plan, or referenced in other standard sources for information generated as part of the system development life cycle. Duplication of information is avoided, whenever possible. The level of detail provided in the security plan is determined by the organization and is typically commensurate with the security categorization of the information system. Information may be added to the system description as it becomes available during the system development life cycle and execution of the RMF tasks. A system description may include, for example:

- Full descriptive name of the information system including associated acronym;
- Unique information system identifier (typically a number or code);
- Information system owner and authorizing official including contact information;

- Parent or governing organization that manages, owns, and/or controls the information system;
- Location of the information system and environment in which the system operates;
- Version or release number of the information system;
- Purpose, functions, and capabilities of the information system and missions/business processes supported;
- How the information system is integrated into the enterprise architecture and information security architecture;
- Status of the information system with respect to acquisition and/or system development life cycle;
- Results of the security categorization process for the information and information system;
- Types of information processed, stored, and transmitted by the information system;
- Boundary of the information system for risk management and security authorization purposes;
- Applicable laws, directives, policies, regulations, or standards affecting the security of the information system;
- Architectural description of the information system including network topology;
- Hardware and firmware devices included within the information system;
- System and applications software resident on the information system;
- Hardware, software, and system interfaces (internal and external);
- Subsystems (static and dynamic) associated with the information system;
- Information flows and paths (including inputs and outputs) within the information system;
- Cross domain devices/requirements;
- Network connection rules for communicating with external information systems;
- Interconnected information systems and identifiers for those systems;
- Encryption techniques used for information processing, transmission, and storage;
- Cryptographic key management information (public key infrastructures, certificate authorities, etc.);
- Information system users (including organizational affiliations, access rights, privileges, citizenship, if applicable);
- Ownership/operation of information system (e.g., government-owned, government-operated; government-owned, contractor-operated; contractor-owned, contractor-operated; nonfederal [state and local governments, grantees]);
- Security authorization date and authorization termination date;
- Incident response points of contact; and
- Other information as required by the organization.

References: None.

INFORMATION SYSTEM REGISTRATION

TASK 1-3: Register the information system with appropriate organizational program/management offices.

Primary Responsibility: Information System Owner.

Supporting Roles: Information System Security Officer.

System Development Life Cycle Phase: Initiation (concept/requirements definition).

Supplemental Guidance: The *registration* process begins by identifying the information system (and subsystems, if appropriate) in the system inventory and establishes a relationship between the information system and the parent or governing organization that owns, manages, and/or controls the system. Information system registration, in accordance with organizational policy, uses information in the system identification section of the security plan to inform the parent or governing organization of: (i) the existence of the information system; (ii) the key characteristics of the system; and (iii) any security implications for the organization due to the ongoing operation of the system. Information system registration provides organizations with an effective management/tracking tool that is necessary for security status reporting in accordance with applicable laws, Executive Orders, directives, policies, standards, guidance, or regulations. Those subsystems that are more dynamic in nature (e.g., subsystems in net-centric architectures) may not be present throughout all phases of the system development life cycle. Such subsystems are registered either as a subset of a well-defined information system or a method of registration for dynamic subsystems is implemented that includes as much information as feasible. Some information about dynamic subsystems is known prior to the subsystem manifesting itself in the information system (e.g., assumptions and constraints specified in the security plan). However, more detailed information may not be known until the subsystem manifests itself.

References: None.

Milestone Checkpoint #1

- Has the organization completed a ***security categorization*** of the information system (informed by the initial risk assessment) including the information to be processed, stored, and transmitted by the system?
- Are the results of the security categorization process for the information system consistent with the organization's ***enterprise architecture*** and commitment to ***protecting organizational mission/business processes***?
- Do the results of the security categorization process reflect the organization's ***risk management strategy***?
- Has the organization adequately described the ***characteristics*** of the information system?
- Has the organization ***registered*** the information system for purposes of management, accountability, coordination, and oversight?

3.2   RMF STEP 2 — SELECT SECURITY CONTROLS

COMMON CONTROL IDENTIFICATION

TASK 2-1: Identify the security controls that are provided by the organization as common controls for organizational information systems and document the controls in a security plan (or equivalent document).

Primary Responsibility: Chief Information Officer or Senior Information Security Officer; Information Security Architect; Common Control Provider.

Supporting Roles: Risk Executive (Function); Authorizing Official or Designated Representative; Information System Owner; Information System Security Engineer.

System Development Life Cycle Phase: Initiation (concept/requirements definition).

Supplemental Guidance: Common controls are security controls that are inherited by one or more organizational information systems. Common controls are identified by the chief information officer and/or senior information security officer in collaboration with the information security architect and assigned to specific organizational entities (designated as common control providers) for development, implementation, assessment, and monitoring. Common control providers may also be *information system owners* when the common controls are resident within an information system. The organization consults information system owners when identifying common controls to ensure that the security capability provided by the inherited controls is sufficient to deliver adequate protection. When the common controls provided by the organization are not sufficient for information systems inheriting the controls, the system owners supplement the common controls with system-specific or hybrid controls to achieve the required protection for the system and/or accept greater risk. Information system owners inheriting common controls can either document the implementation of the controls in their respective security plans or reference the controls contained in the security plans of the common control providers. Organizations may choose to defer common control identification and security control selection until a later phase in the system development life cycle. When common controls are not resident within an information system (e.g., physical and environmental protection controls, personnel security controls), the organization selects one or more senior organizational officials or executives to serve as authorizing officials for those controls. These authorizing officials are responsible for accepting the risk to organizational operations and assets, individuals, other organizations, and the Nation resulting from the deployment of the security controls provided by common control providers and *inherited* by organizational information systems. Common control providers are responsible for: (i) documenting common controls in a *security plan* (or equivalent document prescribed by the organization); (ii) ensuring that common controls are developed, implemented, and assessed for effectiveness by qualified assessors with a level of independence required by the organization; (iii) documenting assessment findings in a *security assessment report*; (iv) producing a *plan of action and milestones* for all common controls deemed less than effective (i.e., having unacceptable weaknesses or deficiencies in the controls); (v) receiving authorization for the common controls from the designated authorizing official; and (vi) monitoring common control effectiveness on an ongoing basis.

Security plans, security assessment reports, and plans of action and milestones for common controls (or a summary of such information) are made available to information system owners (whose systems are *inheriting* the controls) after the information is reviewed and approved by the senior official or executive responsible and accountable for the controls. The organization ensures that common control providers keep this information current since the controls typically support multiple organizational information systems. Security plans, security assessment reports, and plans of action and milestones for common controls are used by authorizing officials within the organization to make risk-based decisions in the security authorization process for their information systems. The use of common controls is documented within the security plans for information systems inheriting those controls. Organizations ensure that common control providers have the capability to rapidly broadcast changes in the status of common controls that adversely affect the protections being provided by and expected of the common controls. Common control providers are able to quickly inform information system owners when problems arise in the inherited common controls (e.g., when an assessment or reassessment of a common control indicates the control is flawed in some manner, when a new threat or attack method arises that renders the common control less than effective in protecting against the new threat or attack method). Organizations are encouraged, when feasible, to employ automated management systems to maintain records of the specific common controls used in each organizational information system to enhance the ability of common control providers to rapidly communicate with information system owners. If common controls are provided to the organization (and its information systems) by entities *external* to the organization (e.g., shared and/or external service providers), arrangements are made with the external/shared service providers by the organization to obtain information on the effectiveness of the deployed controls. Information obtained from external organizations regarding the effectiveness of common controls is factored into authorization decisions.

References: FIPS Publications 199, 200; NIST Special Publications 800-30, 800-53; CNSS Instruction 1253.

SECURITY CONTROL SELECTION

TASK 2-2: Select the security controls for the information system and document the controls in the security plan.

Primary Responsibility: Information Security Architect; Information System Owner.

Supporting Roles: Authorizing Official or Designated Representative; Information Owner/Steward; Information System Security Officer; Information System Security Engineer.

System Development Life Cycle Phase: Initiation (concept/requirements definition).

Supplemental Guidance: The security controls are selected based on the security categorization of the information system. After selecting the applicable security control baseline, organizations apply the tailoring process to align the controls more closely with the specific conditions within the organization (i.e., conditions related to organizational risk tolerance, missions/business functions, information systems, or environments of operation). The tailoring process includes: (i) identifying and designating common controls in initial security control baselines; (ii) applying scoping considerations to the remaining baseline security controls; (iii) selecting compensating security controls, if needed; (iv) assigning specific values to organization-defined security control parameters via explicit assignment and selection statements; (v) supplementing baselines with additional security controls and control enhancements, if needed; and (vi) providing additional specification information for control implementation, if needed. Organizations use risk assessments to inform and guide the tailoring process for organizational information systems and environments of operation. Threat data from risk assessments provide critical information on adversary capabilities, intent, and targeting that may affect organizational decisions regarding the selection of additional security controls, including the associated costs and benefits. Risk assessment results are also leveraged when identifying common controls to help determine if such controls available for inheritance meet the security requirements for the system and its environment of operation (including analyses for potential single points of failure). The security plan contains an overview of the security requirements for the information system in sufficient detail to determine that the security controls selected would meet those requirements. The security plan, in addition to the list of security controls to be implemented, describes the intended application of each control in the context of the information system with sufficient detail to enable a compliant implementation of the control. During the security control selection process organizations may begin planning for the continuous monitoring process by developing a monitoring strategy. The strategy can include, for example, monitoring criteria such as the volatility of specific security controls and the appropriate frequency of monitoring specific controls. Organizations may choose to address security control volatility and frequency of monitoring during control selection as inputs to the continuous monitoring process. The monitoring strategy can be included in the security plan to support the concept of near real-time risk management and ongoing authorization (see Task 2-3). Information system owners *inheriting* common controls can either document the implementation of the controls in their respective security plans or reference the controls contained in the security plans of the common control providers (see Task 2-1). Information system owners can refer to the security authorization packages prepared by common control providers when making determinations regarding the adequacy of common controls inherited by their respective systems.

For net-centric architectures where subsystems may be added or removed from an information system dynamically, the organization includes in the security plan for the system: (i) descriptions of the functions of the dynamic subsystems; (ii) the security controls employed in the subsystems; (iii) constraints/assumptions regarding the functions of the dynamic subsystems and the associated security controls in the subsystems; (iv) dependencies of other subsystems on the proper functioning of the security controls of the dynamic subsystems; (v) procedures for determining that the dynamic subsystems conform to the security plan, assumptions, and constraints; and (vi) the impact of the dynamic subsystems and associated security controls on existing security controls in the information system. While inclusion of a dynamic subsystem may impact the information system or some of the currently identified subsystems, it does not necessarily mean the subsystem will impact the *security* of the system or other subsystems. That is, not all subsystems are security relevant. Changes in the net-centric architectures that exceed the anticipated limits of the security plan may not be allowed or may require reassessment prior to being approved. When security controls are designated as common controls, the organization ensures that sufficient information is available to information system owners and authorizing officials to support the risk management process. When security services are provided by external providers (e.g., through contracts, interagency agreements, lines of business arrangements, licensing agreements, and/or supply chain arrangements), the organization: (i) defines the external services provided to the organization; (ii) describes how the external services are protected in accordance with the security requirements of the organization; and (iii) obtains the necessary assurances that the risk to organizational operations and assets, individuals, other organizations, and the Nation arising from the use of the external services is acceptable. The organization also considers that replicated subsystems within a complex information system may exhibit common vulnerabilities that can be exploited by a common threat source, thereby negating the redundancy that might be relied upon as a risk mitigation measure. The impact due to a security incident against one constituent subsystem might cascade and impact many subsystems at the same time.

References: FIPS Publications 199, 200; NIST Special Publications 800-30, 800-53; CNSS Instruction 1253.

MONITORING STRATEGY

TASK 2-3: Develop a strategy for the continuous monitoring of security control effectiveness and any proposed or actual changes to the information system and its environment of operation.

Primary Responsibility: Information System Owner or Common Control Provider.

Supporting Roles: Risk Executive (Function); Authorizing Official or Designated Representative; Chief Information Officer; Senior Information Security Officer; Information Owner/Steward; Information System Security Officer.

System Development Life Cycle Phase: Initiation (concept/requirements definition).

Supplemental Guidance: A critical aspect of risk management is the ongoing monitoring of security controls employed within or inherited by the information system. An effective monitoring strategy is developed early in the system development life cycle (i.e., during system design or COTS procurement decision) and can be included in the security plan. The implementation of a robust continuous monitoring program allows an organization to understand the security state of the information system over time and maintain the initial security authorization in a highly dynamic environment of operation with changing threats, vulnerabilities, technologies, and missions/business functions. The ongoing monitoring of security controls using automated tools and supporting databases facilitates near real-time risk management for the information system. An effective monitoring program includes: (i) configuration management and control processes; (ii) security impact analyses on proposed or actual changes to the information system and its environment of operation; (iii) assessment of security controls employed within and inherited by the information system (including controls in dynamic subsystems); and (iv) security status reporting to appropriate organizational officials. The continuous monitoring strategy for the information system identifies the security controls to be monitored, the frequency of monitoring, and the control assessment approach. The strategy defines how changes to the information system will be monitored, how security impact analyses will be conducted, and the security status reporting requirements including recipients of the status reports.

The criteria for determining the frequency with which security controls are monitored post deployment is established by the information system owner or common control provider in collaboration with selected organizational officials including, for example, the authorizing official or designated representative, chief information officer, senior information security officer, and risk executive (function). The frequency criteria reflect the priorities and importance of the information system to organizational operations and assets, individuals, other organizations, and the Nation. Security controls that are volatile (i.e., most likely to change over time), critical to certain aspects of the organization's protection strategy, or identified in current plans of action and milestones may require more frequent assessment. The use of automation facilitates a greater frequency and volume of security control assessments.

Determining the frequency for assessing security controls inherited by the information system (i.e., common controls) includes the organization's determination of the trustworthiness of the common control provider. An organizational assessment of risk (either formal or informal) can also be used to guide the frequency of monitoring. The approach to security control assessments during continuous monitoring may include detection of the status of information system components and analysis of historical, operational data, as well as the reuse of assessment procedures and results that supported the initial authorization decision.

The authorizing official or designated representative approve the monitoring strategy including the set of security controls that are to be monitored on an ongoing basis as well as the frequency of the monitoring activities. The approval of the monitoring strategy can be obtained in conjunction with the security plan approval. The monitoring of security controls continues throughout the system development life cycle. For security controls employed in information systems with dynamic subsystems, the monitoring strategy accounts for subsystems that did not exist at the beginning of the system development life cycle. An effective monitoring strategy for dynamic subsystems achieves an appropriate balance with regard to risk by: (i) not placing unnecessary or unrealistic burdens on the organization by requiring reauthorization of the information system each time a new subsystem is added or removed; and (ii) not compromising the accepted security posture of the overall system. NIST Special Publication 800-137 provides additional guidance on continuous monitoring and continuous monitoring strategies.

References: NIST Special Publications 800-30, 800-39, 800-53, 800-53A, 800-137; CNSS Instruction 1253.

SECURITY PLAN APPROVAL

TASK 2-4: Review and approve the security plan.

Primary Responsibility: Authorizing Official or Designated Representative.

Supporting Roles: Risk Executive (Function); Chief Information Officer; Senior Information Security Officer.

System Development Life Cycle Phase: Development/Acquisition.

Supplemental Guidance: The independent review of the security plan by the authorizing official or designated representative with support from the senior information security officer, chief information officer, and risk executive (function), helps determine if the plan is complete, consistent, and satisfies the stated security requirements for the information system. The security plan review also helps to determine, to the greatest extent possible with available planning or operational documents, if the security plan correctly and effectively identifies the potential risk to organizational operations and assets, individuals, other organizations, and the Nation, that would be incurred if the controls identified in the plan were implemented as intended. Based on the results of this independent review and analysis, the authorizing official or designated representative, chief information officer, senior information security officer, or risk executive (function) may recommend changes to the security plan. If the security plan is deemed unacceptable, the authorizing official or designated representative sends the plan back to the information system owner (or common control provider) for appropriate action. If the security plan is deemed acceptable, the authorizing official or designated representative approves the plan. The acceptance of the security plan represents an important milestone in both the risk management process and the system development life cycle. The authorizing official or designated representative, by approving the security plan, agrees to the set of security controls (system-specific, hybrid, and/or common controls) proposed to meet the security requirements for the information system. This approval allows the risk management process to advance to the next step in the RMF (i.e., the implementation of the security controls). The approval of the security plan also establishes the level of effort required to successfully complete the remainder of the steps in the RMF and provides the basis of the security specification for the acquisition of the information system, subsystems, or components.

References: NIST Special Publications 800-30, 800-53; CNSS Instruction 1253.

Milestone Checkpoint #2

- Has the organization allocated all security controls to the *information system* as system-specific, hybrid, or common controls?

- Has the organization used its *risk assessment* (either formal or informal) to inform and guide the security control selection process?

- Has the organization identified *authorizing officials* for the information system and all common controls inherited by the system?

- Has the organization *tailored* the baseline security controls to ensure that the controls, if implemented, adequately mitigate risks to organizational operations and assets, individuals, other organizations, and the Nation?

- Has the organization addressed *minimum assurance requirements* for the security controls employed within and inherited by the information system?

- Has the organization consulted information system owners when *identifying common controls* to ensure that the security capability provided by the inherited controls is sufficient to deliver adequate protection?

- Has the organization *supplemented* the *common controls* with system-specific or hybrid controls when the security control baselines of the common controls are less than those of the information system inheriting the controls?

- Has the organization documented the common controls inherited from *external providers*?

- Has the organization developed a *continuous monitoring strategy* for the information system (including monitoring of security control effectiveness for system-specific, hybrid, and common controls) that reflects the organizational risk management strategy and organizational commitment to protecting critical missions and business functions?

- Have appropriate organizational officials *approved* security plans containing system-specific, hybrid, and common controls?

3.3 RMF STEP 3 – IMPLEMENT SECURITY CONTROLS

SECURITY CONTROL IMPLEMENTATION

TASK 3-1: Implement the security controls specified in the security plan.

Primary Responsibility: Information System Owner or Common Control Provider.

Supporting Roles: Information Owner/Steward; Information System Security Officer; Information System Security Engineer.

System Development Life Cycle Phase: Development/Acquisition; Implementation.

Supplemental Guidance: Security control implementation is consistent with the organization's enterprise architecture and information security architecture. The information security architecture serves as a resource to allocate security controls (including, for example, security mechanisms and services) to an information system and any organization-defined subsystems. Early integration of information security requirements into the system development life cycle is the most cost-effective method for implementing the organizational risk management strategy at Tier 3. Security controls targeted for deployment within the information system (including subsystems) are allocated to specific system components responsible for providing a particular security capability. Not all security controls need to be allocated to every subsystem. Categorization of subsystems, information security architecture, and allocation of security controls work together to help achieve a suitable balance. Allocating some security controls as common controls or hybrid controls is part of this architectural process. Organizations use best practices when implementing the security controls within the information system including system and software engineering methodologies, security engineering principles, and secure coding techniques. Risk assessment may help inform decisions regarding the cost, benefit, and risk trade-offs in using one type of technology versus another for control implementation. In addition, organizations ensure that mandatory configuration settings are established and implemented on information technology products in accordance with federal and organizational policies (e.g., Federal Desktop Core Configuration). Information system security engineers with support from information system security officers employ a sound security engineering process that captures and refines information security requirements and ensures the integration of those requirements into information technology products and systems through purposeful security design or configuration. When available, organizations consider the use of information technology products that have been tested, evaluated, or validated by approved, independent, third-party assessment facilities. In addition, organizations satisfy, where applicable, minimum assurance requirements when implementing security controls. Assurance requirements are directed at the activities and actions that security control developers and implementers define and apply to increase the level of confidence that the controls are implemented correctly, operating as intended, and producing the desired outcome with respect to meeting the security requirements for the information system. Assurance requirements address the quality of the design, development, and implementation of the security functions in the information system. For higher-impact systems (i.e., potential high-value targets) in situations where specific and credible threat information indicates the likelihood of advanced cyber attacks, additional assurance measures are considered. Organizations consider any implementation-related issues associated with the integration and/or interfaces among common controls and system-specific controls.

For the identified common controls inherited by the information system, information system security engineers with support from information system security officers coordinate with the common control provider to determine the most appropriate way to apply the common controls to the organizational information systems. For certain management and operational controls, formal integration into information technology products, services, and systems may not be required. For certain types of operational and/or technical controls, implementation may require additional components, products, or services to enable the information system to utilize the previously selected common controls to the fullest extent. If selection of common controls previously had been deferred, identification of common controls inherited by the information system is revisited to determine if better determinations can be made at this point in the system development life cycle. Information system owners can refer to the authorization packages prepared by common control providers when making determinations regarding the adequacy of the implementations of common controls for their respective systems. For common controls that do not meet the protection needs of the information systems inheriting the controls or that have unacceptable weaknesses or deficiencies, the system owners identify compensating or supplementary controls to be implemented. Risk assessment may help determine how gaps in protection needs between systems and common controls affect the overall risk associated with the system, and how to prioritize the need for compensating or supplementary controls to mitigate specific risks. To the maximum extent and consistent with the flexibility allowed in applying the tasks in the RMF, organizations and their contractors conduct initial security control assessments (also referred to as developmental testing and evaluation) during information system development and implementation. Conducting security control assessments in parallel with the development and implementation phases of the system development life cycle facilitates the early identification of weaknesses and deficiencies and provides the most cost-effective method for initiating corrective actions. Issues found during these assessments can be referred to authorizing officials for early resolution, as appropriate. The results of the initial security control assessments can also be used during the security authorization process to avoid delays or costly repetition of assessments. Assessment results that are subsequently reused in other phases of the system development life cycle meet the reuse requirements (including independence) established by the organization.

References: FIPS Publication 200; NIST Special Publications 800-30, 800-53, 800-53A; CNSS Instruction 1253; Web: SCAP.NIST.GOV.

SECURITY CONTROL DOCUMENTATION

TASK 3-2: Document the security control implementation, as appropriate, in the security plan, providing a functional description of the control implementation (including planned inputs, expected behavior, and expected outputs).

Primary Responsibility: Information System Owner or Common Control Provider.

Supporting Roles: Information Owner/Steward; Information System Security Officer; Information System Security Engineer.

System Development Life Cycle Phase: Development/Acquisition; Implementation.

Supplemental Guidance: Security control documentation describes how system-specific, hybrid, and common controls are implemented. The documentation formalizes plans and expectations regarding the overall functionality of the information system. The functional description of the security control implementation includes planned inputs, expected behavior, and expected outputs where appropriate, typically for those technical controls that are employed in the hardware, software, or firmware components of the information system. Documentation of security control implementation allows for traceability of decisions prior to and after deployment of the information system. The level of effort expended on documentation of the information system is commensurate with the purpose, scope, and impact of the system with respect to organizational missions, business functions, and operations. To the extent possible, organizations reference existing documentation (either by vendors or other organizations that have employed the same or similar information systems), use automated support tools, and maximize communications to increase the overall efficiency and cost effectiveness of security control implementation. The documentation also addresses platform dependencies and includes any additional information necessary to describe how the security capability required by the security control is achieved at the level of detail sufficient to support control assessment. Documentation for security control implementation follows best practices for hardware and software development as well as for system/security engineering disciplines and is consistent with established organizational policies and procedures for documenting system development life cycle activities. Whenever possible and practicable for technical security controls that are mechanism-based, organizations take maximum advantage of functional specifications provided by or obtainable from hardware and software vendors and/or systems integrators including security-relevant documentation that may assist the organization during the assessment and monitoring of the controls. Similarly, for management and operational controls, organizations obtain security control implementation information from appropriate organizational entities (e.g., facilities offices, human resource offices, physical security offices). Since the enterprise architecture and information security architecture established by the organization significantly influence the approach used to implement security controls, providing documentation of this process helps to ensure traceability with regard to meeting the organization's information security requirements.

References: NIST Special Publication 800-53; CNSS Instruction 1253.

Milestone Checkpoint #3

- Has the organization *allocated* security controls as system-specific, hybrid, or common controls consistent with the enterprise architecture and information security architecture?

- Has the organization demonstrated the use of sound *information system and security engineering methodologies* in integrating information technology products into the information system and in implementing the security controls contained in the security plan?

- Has the organization documented how *common controls* inherited by organizational information systems have been implemented?

- Has the organization documented how *system-specific* and *hybrid* security controls have been implemented within the information system taking into account specific technologies and platform dependencies?

- Has the organization taken into account the *minimum assurance requirements* when implementing security controls?

3.4 RMF STEP 4 — ASSESS SECURITY CONTROLS

ASSESSMENT PREPARATION

TASK 4-1: Develop, review, and approve a plan to assess the security controls.

Primary Responsibility: Security Control Assessor.

Supporting Roles: Authorizing Official or Designated Representative; Chief Information Officer; Senior Information Security Officer; Information System Owner or Common Control Provider; Information Owner/Steward; Information System Security Officer.

System Development Life Cycle Phase: Development/Acquisition; Implementation.

Supplemental Guidance: The *security assessment plan* provides the objectives for the security control assessment, a detailed roadmap of how to conduct such an assessment, and assessment procedures. The assessment plan reflects the type of assessment the organization is conducting (e.g., developmental testing and evaluation, independent verification and validation, assessments supporting security authorizations or reauthorizations, audits, continuous monitoring, assessments subsequent to remediation actions). Conducting security control assessments in parallel with the development/acquisition and implementation phases of the life cycle permits the identification of weaknesses and deficiencies early and provides the most cost-effective method for initiating corrective actions. Issues found during these assessments can be referred to authorizing officials for early resolution, as appropriate. The results of security control assessments carried out during system development and implementation can also be used (consistent with reuse criteria) during the security authorization process to avoid system fielding delays or costly repetition of assessments. The security assessment plan is reviewed and approved by appropriate organizational officials to ensure that the plan is consistent with the security objectives of the organization, employs state-of-the practice tools, techniques, procedures, and automation to support the concept of continuous monitoring and near real-time risk management, and is cost-effective with regard to the resources allocated for the assessment. The purpose of the security assessment plan approval is two-fold: (i) to establish the appropriate expectations for the security control assessment; and (ii) to bound the level of effort for the security control assessment. An approved security assessment plan helps to ensure that an appropriate level of resources is applied toward determining security control effectiveness. When security controls are provided to an organization by an external provider (e.g., through contracts, interagency agreements, lines of business arrangements, licensing agreements, and/or supply chain arrangements), the organization obtains a security assessment plan from the provider.

Organizations consider both the *technical expertise* and level of *independence* required in selecting security control assessors. Organizations also ensure that security control assessors possess the required skills and technical expertise to successfully carry out assessments of system-specific, hybrid, and common controls. This includes knowledge of and experience with the specific hardware, software, and firmware components employed by the organization. An independent assessor is any individual or group capable of conducting an impartial assessment of security controls employed within or inherited by an information system. Impartiality implies that assessors are free from any perceived or actual conflicts of interest with respect to the development, operation, and/or management of the information system or the determination of security control effectiveness. Independent security control assessment services can be obtained from other elements within the organization or can be contracted to a public or private sector entity outside of the organization. Contracted assessment services are considered independent if the information system owner is not directly involved in the contracting process or cannot unduly influence the independence of the assessor(s) conducting the assessment of the security controls. The authorizing official or designated representative determines the required level of independence for security control assessors based on the results of the security categorization process for the information system and the ultimate risk to organizational operations and assets, individuals, other organizations, and the Nation. The authorizing official determines if the level of assessor independence is sufficient to provide confidence that the assessment results produced are sound and can be used to support a risk-based decision on whether to place the information system into operation or continue its operation. In special situations, for example when the organization that owns the information system is small or the organizational structure requires that the security control assessment be accomplished by individuals that are in the developmental, operational, and/or management chain of the system owner, independence in the assessment process can be achieved by ensuring that the assessment results are carefully reviewed and analyzed by an independent team of experts to validate the completeness, consistency, and veracity of the results. The authorizing official consults with the Office of the Inspector General, the senior information security officer, and the chief information officer to discuss the implications of any decisions on assessor independence in the types of special circumstances described above. This discussion may occur prior to each security assessment or only once if an organization is establishing an organizational policy and approach for specific special circumstances that will be applied to all information systems meeting the specific special circumstance criteria. Security control assessments in support of initial and subsequent security authorizations are conducted by independent assessors.

References: NIST Special Publication 800-53A.

SECURITY CONTROL ASSESSMENT

TASK 4-2: Assess the security controls in accordance with the assessment procedures defined in the security assessment plan.

Primary Responsibility: Security Control Assessor.

Supporting Roles: Information System Owner or Common Control Provider; Information Owner/Steward; Information System Security Officer.

System Development Life Cycle Phase: Development/Acquisition; Implementation.

Supplemental Guidance: Security control assessments determine the extent to which the controls are implemented correctly, operating as intended, and producing the desired outcome with respect to meeting the security requirements for the information system. Security control assessments occur as early as practicable in the system development life cycle, preferably during the development phase of the information system. These types of assessments are referred to as *developmental testing and evaluation* and are intended to validate that the required security controls are implemented correctly and consistent with the established information security architecture. Developmental testing and evaluation activities include, for example, design and code reviews, application scanning, and regression testing. Security weaknesses and deficiencies identified early in the system development life cycle can be resolved more quickly and in a much more cost-effective manner before proceeding to subsequent phases in the life cycle. The objective is to identify the information security architecture and security controls up front and to ensure that the system design and testing validate the implementation of these controls.

The information system owner relies on the technical expertise and judgment of assessors to: (i) assess the security controls employed within or inherited by the information system using assessment procedures specified in the security assessment plan; and (ii) provide specific recommendations on how to correct weaknesses or deficiencies in the controls and reduce or eliminate identified vulnerabilities. The assessor findings are an unbiased, factual reporting of the weaknesses and deficiencies discovered during the security control assessment. Organizations are encouraged to maximize the use of automation to conduct security control assessments to help: (i) increase the speed and overall effectiveness and efficiency of the assessments; and (ii) support the concept of ongoing monitoring of the security state of organizational information systems. When iterative development processes such as agile development are employed, this typically results in an iterative assessment as each cycle is conducted. A similar process is used for assessing security controls in COTS information technology products employed within the information system. Even when iterative development is not employed, organizations may choose to begin assessing security controls prior to the complete implementation of all security controls listed in the security plan. This type of *incremental assessment* is appropriate if it is more efficient or cost-effective to do so. For example, policy, procedures, and plans may be assessed prior to the assessment of the technical security controls in the hardware and software. In many cases, common controls (i.e., security controls inherited by the information system) may be assessed prior to the security controls employed within the system.

The organization ensures that assessors have access to: (i) the information system and environment of operation where the security controls are employed; and (ii) the appropriate documentation, records, artifacts, test results, and other materials needed to assess the security controls. In addition, assessors have the required degree of independence as determined by the authorizing official (see Appendix D.13 and Appendix F.4). Security control assessments in support of initial and subsequent security authorizations are conducted by independent assessors. Assessor independence during continuous monitoring, although not mandated, facilitates reuse of assessment results when reauthorization is required. When security controls are provided to an organization by an external provider (e.g., through contracts, interagency agreements, lines of business arrangements, licensing agreements, and/or supply chain arrangements), the organization ensures that assessors have access to the information system/environment of operation where the controls are employed as well as appropriate information needed to carry out the assessment. The organization also obtains any information related to existing assessments that may have been conducted by the external provider and reuses such assessment information whenever possible in accordance with the reuse criteria established by the organization. Descriptive information about the information system is typically documented in the system identification section of the security plan or included by reference or as attachments to the plan. Supporting materials such as procedures, reports, logs, and records showing evidence of security control implementation are identified as well. In order to make the risk management process as timely and cost-effective as possible, the reuse of previous assessment results, when reasonable and appropriate, is strongly recommended. For example, a recent audit of an information system may have produced information about the effectiveness of selected security controls. Another opportunity to reuse previous assessment results comes from programs that test and evaluate the security features of commercial information technology products. Additionally, if prior assessment results from the system developer are available, the security control assessor, under appropriate circumstances, may incorporate those results into the assessment. And finally, assessment results are reused to support reciprocity where possible.

References: NIST Special Publication 800-53A.

SECURITY ASSESSMENT REPORT

TASK 4-3: Prepare the security assessment report documenting the issues, findings, and recommendations from the security control assessment.

Primary Responsibility: Security Control Assessor.

Supporting Roles: Information System Owner or Common Control Provider; Information System Security Officer.

System Development Life Cycle Phase: Development/Acquisition; Implementation.

Supplemental Guidance: The results of the security control assessment, including recommendations for correcting any weaknesses or deficiencies in the controls, are documented in the *security assessment report*. The security assessment report is one of three key documents in the security authorization package developed for authorizing officials. The assessment report includes information from the assessor necessary to determine the effectiveness of the security controls employed within or inherited by the information system based upon the assessor's findings. The security assessment report is an important factor in an authorizing official's determination of risk to organizational operations and assets, individuals, other organizations, and the Nation. Security control assessment results are documented at a level of detail appropriate for the assessment in accordance with the reporting format prescribed by organizational and/or federal policies. The reporting format is also appropriate for the type of security control assessment conducted (e.g., developmental testing and evaluation, self-assessments, independent verification and validation, independent assessments supporting the security authorization process or subsequent reauthorizations, assessments during continuous monitoring, assessments subsequent to remediation actions, independent audits/evaluations).

Security control assessment results obtained during system development are brought forward in an interim report and included in the final security assessment report. This supports the concept that the security assessment report is an evolving document that includes assessment results from all relevant phases of the system development life cycle including the results generated during continuous monitoring. Organizations may choose to develop an *executive summary* from the detailed findings that are generated during a security control assessment. An executive summary provides an authorizing official with an abbreviated version of the assessment report focusing on the highlights of the assessment, synopsis of key findings, and/or recommendations for addressing weaknesses and deficiencies in the security controls.

References: NIST Special Publication 800-53A.

REMEDIATION ACTIONS

TASK 4-4: Conduct initial remediation actions on security controls based on the findings and recommendations of the security assessment report and reassess remediated control(s), as appropriate.

Primary Responsibility: Information System Owner or Common Control Provider; Security Control Assessor.

Supporting Roles: Authorizing Official or Designated Representative; Chief Information Officer; Senior Information Security Officer; Information Owner/Steward; Information System Security Officer; Information System Security Engineer; Security Control Assessor.

System Development Life Cycle Phase: Development/Acquisition; Implementation.

Supplemental Guidance: The security assessment report provides visibility into specific weaknesses and deficiencies in the security controls employed within or inherited by the information system that could not reasonably be resolved during system development or that are discovered post-development. Such weaknesses and deficiencies are potential vulnerabilities if exploitable by a threat source. The findings generated during the security control assessment provide important information that facilitates a disciplined and structured approach to mitigating risks in accordance with organizational priorities. An updated assessment of risk (either formal or informal) based on the results of the findings produced during the security control assessment and any inputs from the risk executive (function), helps to determine the initial remediation actions and the prioritization of such actions. Information system owners and common control providers, in collaboration with selected organizational officials (e.g., information system security engineer, authorizing official designated representative, chief information officer, senior information security officer, information owner/steward), may decide, based on an initial or updated assessment of risk, that certain findings are inconsequential and present no significant risk to the organization. Alternatively, the organizational officials may decide that certain findings are in fact, significant, requiring immediate remediation actions. In all cases, organizations review assessor findings and determine the severity or seriousness of the findings (i.e., the potential adverse impact on organizational operations and assets, individuals, other organizations, or the Nation) and whether the findings are sufficiently significant to be worthy of further investigation or remediation. Senior leadership involvement in the mitigation process may be necessary in order to ensure that the organization's resources are effectively allocated in accordance with organizational priorities, providing resources first to the information systems that are supporting the most critical and sensitive missions and business functions for the organization or correcting the deficiencies that pose the greatest degree of risk. If weaknesses or deficiencies in security controls are corrected, the security control assessor reassesses the remediated controls for effectiveness. Security control reassessments determine the extent to which the remediated controls are implemented correctly, operating as intended, and producing the desired outcome with respect to meeting the security requirements for the information system. Exercising caution not to change the original assessment results, assessors update the security assessment report with the findings from the reassessment. The security plan is updated based on the findings of the security control assessment and any remediation actions taken. The updated security plan reflects the actual state of the security controls after the initial assessment and any modifications by the information system owner or common control provider in addressing recommendations for corrective actions. At the completion of the assessment, the security plan contains an accurate list and description of the security controls implemented (including compensating controls) and a list of residual vulnerabilities.

Organizations can prepare an optional addendum to the security assessment report that is transmitted to the authorizing official. The optional addendum provides information system owners and common control providers an opportunity to respond to the initial findings of assessors. The addendum may include, for example, information regarding initial remediation actions taken by information system owners or common control providers in response to assessor findings, or provide an owner's perspective on the findings (e.g., including additional explanatory material, rebutting certain findings, and correcting the record). The addendum to the security assessment report does not change or influence in any manner, the initial assessor findings provided in the original report. Information provided in the addendum is considered by authorizing officials in their risk-based authorization decisions. Organizations may choose to employ an *issue resolution process* to help determine the appropriate actions to take with regard to the security control weaknesses and deficiencies identified during the assessment. Issue resolution can help address vulnerabilities and associated risk, false positives, and other factors that may provide useful information to authorizing officials regarding the security state of the information system including the ongoing effectiveness of system-specific, hybrid, and common controls. The issue resolution process can also help to ensure that only substantive items are identified and transferred to the plan of actions and milestones.

References: NIST Special Publications 800-30, 800-53A.

Milestone Checkpoint #4

- Has the organization developed a comprehensive *plan* to assess the security controls employed within or inherited by the information system?

- Was the assessment plan *reviewed* and *approved* by appropriate organizational officials?

- Has the organization considered the appropriate level of assessor *independence* for the security control assessment?

- Has the organization provided all of the essential supporting *assessment-related materials* needed by the assessor(s) to conduct an effective security control assessment?

- Has the organization examined opportunities for *reusing assessment results* from previous assessments or from other sources?

- Did the assessor(s) complete the *security control assessment* in accordance with the stated assessment plan?

- Did the organization receive the completed *security assessment report* with appropriate findings and recommendations from the assessor(s)?

- Did the organization take the necessary *remediation actions* to address the most important weaknesses and deficiencies in the information system and its environment of operation based on the findings and recommendations in the security assessment report?

- Did the assessor *reassess the remediated controls* for effectiveness to provide the authorization official with an unbiased, factual security assessment report on the weaknesses or deficiencies in the system?

- Did the organization update appropriate *security plans* based on the findings and recommendations in the security assessment report and any subsequent changes to the information system and its environment of operation?

3.5 RMF STEP 5 – AUTHORIZE INFORMATION SYSTEM

PLAN OF ACTION AND MILESTONES

TASK 5-1: Prepare the plan of action and milestones based on the findings and recommendations of the security assessment report excluding any remediation actions taken.

Primary Responsibility: Information System Owner or Common Control Provider.

Supporting Roles: Information Owner/Steward; Information System Security Officer.

System Development Life Cycle Phase: Implementation.

Supplemental Guidance: The *plan of action and milestones*, prepared for the authorizing official by the information system owner or the common control provider, is one of three key documents in the security authorization package and describes the specific tasks that are planned: (i) to correct any weaknesses or deficiencies in the security controls noted during the assessment; and (ii) to address the residual vulnerabilities in the information system. The plan of action and milestones identifies: (i) the tasks to be accomplished with a recommendation for completion either before or after information system implementation; (ii) the resources required to accomplish the tasks; (iii) any milestones in meeting the tasks; and (iv) the scheduled completion dates for the milestones. The plan of action and milestones is used by the authorizing official to monitor progress in correcting weaknesses or deficiencies noted during the security control assessment. All security weaknesses and deficiencies identified during the security control assessment are documented in the security assessment report to maintain an effective audit trail. Organizations develop specific plans of action and milestones based on the results of the security control assessment and in accordance with applicable laws, Executive Orders, directives, policies, standards, guidance, or regulations. Plan of action and milestones entries are *not* required when weaknesses or deficiencies are remediated during the assessment or prior to the submission of the authorization package to the authorizing official.

Organizations define a strategy for developing plans of action and milestones that facilitates a prioritized approach to risk mitigation that is consistent across the organization. The strategy helps to ensure that organizational plans of action and milestones are based on: (i) the security categorization of the information system; (ii) the specific weaknesses or deficiencies in the security controls; (iii) the importance of the identified security control weaknesses or deficiencies (i.e., the direct or indirect effect the weaknesses or deficiencies may have on the overall security state of the information system, and hence on the risk exposure of the organization, or ability of the organization to perform its mission or business functions); and (iv) the organization's proposed risk mitigation approach to address the identified weaknesses or deficiencies in the security controls (e.g., prioritization of risk mitigation actions, allocation of risk mitigation resources). A risk assessment guides the prioritization process for items included in the plan of action and milestones.

References: OMB Memorandum 02-01; NIST Special Publications 800-30, 800-53A.

SECURITY AUTHORIZATION PACKAGE

TASK 5-2: Assemble the security authorization package and submit the package to the authorizing official for adjudication.

Primary Responsibility: Information System Owner or Common Control Provider.

Supporting Roles: Information System Security Officer; Security Control Assessor.

System Development Life Cycle Phase: Implementation.

Supplemental Guidance: The *security authorization package* contains: (i) the security plan; (ii) the security assessment report; and (iii) the plan of action and milestones. The information in these key documents is used by authorizing officials to make risk-based authorization decisions. For information systems inheriting common controls for specific security capabilities, the security authorization package for the common controls or a reference to such documentation is also included in the authorization package. When security controls are provided to an organization by an external provider (e.g., through contracts, interagency agreements, lines of business arrangements, licensing agreements, and/or supply chain arrangements), the organization ensures that the information needed for authorizing officials to make risk-based decisions, is made available by the provider.

Additional information can be included in the security authorization package at the request of the authorizing official carrying out the authorization action. The contents of the security authorization package are protected appropriately in accordance with federal and organizational policies. Organizations are strongly encouraged to use automated support tools in preparing and managing the content of the security authorization package to help provide an effective vehicle for maintaining and updating information for authorizing officials regarding the ongoing security status of information systems within the organization. Providing orderly, disciplined, and timely updates to the security plan, security assessment report, and plan of action and milestones on an ongoing basis, supports the concept of near real-time risk management and ongoing authorization. It also facilitates more cost-effective and meaningful reauthorization actions, if required. Organizations maintain strict version control as key documents in the authorization package are updated. With the use of automated tools and supporting databases, authorizing officials and other senior leaders within the organization are able to maintain awareness with regard to the security state of the information system including the ongoing effectiveness of system-specific, hybrid, and common controls.

References: None.

RISK DETERMINATION

TASK 5-3: Determine the risk to organizational operations (including mission, functions, image, or reputation), organizational assets, individuals, other organizations, or the Nation.

Primary Responsibility: Authorizing Official or Designated Representative.

Supporting Roles: Risk Executive (Function); Senior Information Security Officer.

System Development Life Cycle Phase: Implementation.

Supplemental Guidance: The authorizing official or designated representative, in collaboration with the senior information security officer, assesses the information provided by the information system owner or common control provider regarding the current security state of the system or the common controls inherited by the system and the recommendations for addressing any residual risks. Risk assessments (either formal or informal) are employed at the discretion of the organization to provide needed information on threats, vulnerabilities, and potential impacts as well as the analyses for the risk mitigation recommendations. The risk executive (function) also provides information to the authorizing official that is considered in the final determination of risk to organizational operations and assets, individuals, other organizations, and the Nation resulting from the operation and use of the information system. Risk-related information includes the criticality of organizational missions and/or business functions supported by the information system and the risk management strategy for the organization. The risk management strategy typically describes: (i) how risk is assessed within the organization (i.e., tools, techniques, procedures, and methodologies); (ii) how assessed risks are evaluated with regard to severity or criticality; (iii) known existing aggregated risks from organizational information systems and other sources; (iv) risk response approaches; (v) organizational risk tolerance; and (vi) how risk is monitored over time. When making the final risk determination, the authorizing official or designated representative considers information obtained from the risk executive (function) and the information provided by the information system owner or common control provider in the security authorization package (i.e., security plan, security assessment report, and plan of action and milestones). Conversely, information system-related security risk information derived from the execution of the RMF is available to the risk executive (function) for use in formulating and updating the organization-wide risk management strategy. After risk determination, organizations can respond to risk in a variety of ways, including: (i) accepting risk; (ii) avoiding risk; (iii) mitigating risk; (iv) sharing risk; (v) transferring risk; or (vi) a combination of the above. Decisions on the most appropriate course of action for risk response include some form of prioritization. Some risks may be of greater concern than other risks. In that case, more resources may need to be directed at addressing higher-priority risks than at other lower-priority risks. This does not necessarily mean that the lower-priority risks are ignored. Rather, it could mean that fewer resources are directed at the lower-priority risks (at least initially), or that the lower-priority risks are addressed at a later time. A key part of the risk decision process is the recognition that regardless of the risk decision, there typically remains a degree of residual risk. Organizations determine acceptable degrees of residual risk based on organizational risk tolerance.

References: NIST Special Publications 800-30, 800-39.

RISK ACCEPTANCE

TASK 5-4: Determine if the risk to organizational operations, organizational assets, individuals, other organizations, or the Nation is acceptable.

Primary Responsibility: Authorizing Official.

Supporting Roles: Risk Executive (Function); Authorizing Official Designated Representative; Senior Information Security Officer.

System Development Life Cycle Phase: Implementation.

Supplemental Guidance: The explicit acceptance of *risk* is the responsibility of the authorizing official and cannot be delegated to other officials within the organization. The authorizing official considers many factors when deciding if the risk to organizational operations (including mission, function, image, or reputation), organizational assets, individuals, other organizations, and the Nation, is acceptable. Balancing security considerations with mission and operational needs is paramount to achieving an acceptable authorization decision. The authorizing official issues an authorization decision for the information system and the common controls inherited by the system after reviewing all of the relevant information and, where appropriate, consulting with other organizational officials, including the organization's risk executive (function). Security authorization decisions are based on the content of the security authorization package and, where appropriate, any inputs received from key organizational officials, including the risk executive (function). The authorization package provides relevant information on the security state of the information system including the ongoing effectiveness of the security controls employed within or inherited by the system. Inputs from the risk executive (function), including previously established overarching risk guidance to authorizing officials, provide additional organization-wide information to the authorizing official that may be relevant and affect the authorization decision (e.g., organizational risk tolerance, specific mission and business requirements, dependencies among information systems, and other types of risks not directly associated with the information system). Risk executive (function) inputs are documented and become part of the security authorization decision. Security authorization decisions, including inputs from the risk executive (function), are conveyed to information system owners and common control providers and made available to interested parties within the organization (e.g., information system owners and authorizing officials for interconnected systems, chief information officers, information owners/stewards, senior managers).

The *authorization decision document* conveys the final security authorization decision from the authorizing official to the information system owner or common control provider, and other organizational officials, as appropriate. The authorization decision document contains the following information: (i) authorization decision; (ii) terms and conditions for the authorization; and (iii) authorization termination date. The security *authorization decision* indicates to the information system owner whether the system is: (i) authorized to operate; or (ii) not authorized to operate. The *terms and conditions* for the authorization provide a description of any specific limitations or restrictions placed on the operation of the information system or inherited controls that must be followed by the system owner or common control provider. The *authorization termination date*, established by the authorizing official, indicates when the security authorization expires. Authorization termination dates are influenced by federal and/or organizational policies which may establish maximum authorization periods. Organizations may choose to eliminate the authorization termination date if the continuous monitoring program is sufficiently robust to provide the authorizing official with the needed information to conduct ongoing risk determination and risk acceptance activities with regard to the security state of the information system and the ongoing effectiveness of security controls employed within and inherited by the system.

If the security control assessments are conducted by qualified assessors with the required degree of *independence* based on federal/organizational policies, appropriate security standards and guidelines, and the needs of the authorizing official, the assessment results can be cumulatively applied to the reauthorization, thus supporting the concept of ongoing authorization. Organizational policies regarding ongoing authorization and formal reauthorization, if/when required, are consistent with federal directives, regulations, and/or policies.

The authorization decision document is attached to the original security authorization package containing the supporting documentation and transmitted to the information system owner or common control provider. Upon receipt of the authorization decision document and original authorization package, the information system owner or common control provider acknowledges and implements the terms and conditions of the authorization and notifies the authorizing official. The organization ensures that authorization documents for both information systems and for common controls are made available to appropriate organizational officials (e.g., information system owners inheriting common controls, risk executive (function), chief information officers, senior information security officers, information system security officers). Authorization documents, especially information dealing with information system vulnerabilities, are: (i) marked and appropriately protected in accordance with federal and organizational policies; and (ii) retained in accordance with the organization's record retention policy. The authorizing official verifies, on an ongoing basis, that the terms and conditions established as part of the authorization are being followed by the information system owner or common control provider.

References: NIST Special Publication 800-39.

Milestone Checkpoint #5

- Did the organization develop a ***plan of action and milestones*** reflecting organizational priorities for addressing the remaining weaknesses and deficiencies in the information system and its environment of operation?

- Did the organization develop an appropriate ***authorization package*** with all key documents including the security plan, security assessment report, and plan of action and milestones (if applicable)?

- Did the final ***risk determination*** and ***risk acceptance*** by the authorizing official reflect the risk management strategy developed by the organization and conveyed by the risk executive (function)?

- Was the ***authorization decision*** conveyed to appropriate organizational personnel including information system owners and common control providers?

3.6 RMF STEP 6 – MONITOR SECURITY CONTROLS

INFORMATION SYSTEM AND ENVIRONMENT CHANGES

TASK 6-1: Determine the security impact of proposed or actual changes to the information system and its environment of operation.

Primary Responsibility: Information System Owner or Common Control Provider.

Supporting Roles: Risk Executive (Function); Authorizing Official or Designated Representative; Senior Information Security Officer; Information Owner/Steward; Information System Security Officer.

System Development Life Cycle Phase: Operation/Maintenance.

Supplemental Guidance: Information systems are in a constant state of change with upgrades to hardware, software, or firmware and modifications to the surrounding environments where the systems reside and operate. A disciplined and structured approach to managing, controlling, and documenting changes to an information system or its environment of operation is an essential element of an effective security control monitoring program. Strict configuration management and control processes are established by the organization to support such monitoring activities. It is important to record any relevant information about specific changes to hardware, software, or firmware such as version or release numbers, descriptions of new or modified features/capabilities, and security implementation guidance. It is also important to record any changes to the environment of operation for the information system (e.g., modifications to hosting networks and facilities, mission/business use of the system, threats), or changes to the organizational risk management strategy. The information system owner and common control provider use this information in assessing the potential security impact of the changes. Documenting proposed or actual changes to an information system or its environment of operation and subsequently assessing the potential impact those changes may have on the security state of the system or the organization is an important aspect of security control monitoring and maintaining the security authorization over time. Information system changes are generally not undertaken prior to assessing the security impact of such changes. Organizations are encouraged to maximize the use of automation when managing changes to the information system or its environment of operation.

Security impact analysis conducted by the organization, determines the extent to which proposed or actual changes to the information system or its environment of operation can affect or have affected the security state of the system. Changes to the information system or its environment of operation may affect the security controls currently in place (including system-specific, hybrid, and common controls), produce new vulnerabilities in the system, or generate requirements for new security controls that were not needed previously. If the results of the security impact analysis indicate that the proposed or actual changes can affect or have affected the security state of the system, corrective actions are initiated and appropriate documents revised and updated (e.g., the security plan, security assessment report, and plan of action and milestones). The information system owner or common control provider consults with appropriate organizational officials/entities (e.g., configuration control board, senior information security officer, information system security officer) prior to implementing any security-related changes to the information system or its environment of operation. The authorizing official or designated representative uses the revised and updated security assessment report in collaboration with the senior information security officer and risk executive (function) to determine if a formal reauthorization action is necessary. Most routine changes to an information system or its environment of operation can be handled by the organization's continuous monitoring program, thus supporting the concept of ongoing authorization and near real-time risk management. Conducting security impact analyses is part of an ongoing assessment of risk. As risk assessments are updated and refined, organizations use the results to modify security plans based on the most recent threat and vulnerability information available. Updated risk assessments provide a foundation for prioritizing/planning risk responses. The authorizing official or designated representative, in collaboration with the risk executive (function), confirms as needed, determinations of residual risk. The risk executive (function) notifies the authorizing official of any significant changes in the organizational risk posture.

References: NIST Special Publications 800-30, 800-53A.

ONGOING SECURITY CONTROL ASSESSMENTS

TASK 6-2: Assess the technical, management, and operational security controls employed within and inherited by the information system in accordance with the organization-defined monitoring strategy.

Primary Responsibility: Security Control Assessor.

Supporting Roles: Authorizing Official or Designated Representative; Information System Owner or Common Control Provider; Information Owner/Steward; Information System Security Officer.

System Development Life Cycle Phase: Operation/Maintenance.

Supplemental Guidance: Subsequent to the initial authorization (i.e., during continuous monitoring), the organization assesses all security controls (including management, operational, and technical controls) employed within and inherited by the information system on an ongoing basis. The frequency of monitoring is based on the monitoring strategy developed by the information system owner or common control provider and approved by the authorizing official and senior information security officer. For ongoing security control assessments, assessors have the required degree of independence as determined by the authorizing official (see Appendix D.13 and Appendix F.4). Security control assessments in support of initial and subsequent security authorizations are conducted by independent assessors. Assessor independence during continuous monitoring, although not mandated, introduces efficiencies into the process and allows for reuse of assessment results in support of ongoing authorization and when reauthorization is required. Organizations can use the current year's assessment results to meet the annual FISMA security control assessment requirement. To satisfy this requirement, organizations can draw upon the assessment results from any of the following sources, including but not limited to: (i) security control assessments conducted as part of an information system authorization, ongoing authorization, or formal reauthorization, if required; (ii) continuous monitoring activities; or (iii) testing and evaluation of the information system as part of the system development life cycle process or audit (provided that the testing, evaluation, or audit results are current, relevant to the determination of security control effectiveness, and obtained by assessors with the required degree of independence). Existing security assessment results are reused to the extent that they are still valid and are supplemented with additional assessments as needed. Reuse of assessment information is critical in achieving a cost-effective, fully integrated security program capable of producing the needed evidence to determine the security status of the information system. The use of automation to support security control assessments facilitates a greater frequency and volume of assessments that is consistent with the monitoring strategy established by the organization.

References: NIST Special Publications 800-53A, 800-137.

ONGOING REMEDIATION ACTIONS

TASK 6-3: Conduct remediation actions based on the results of ongoing monitoring activities, assessment of risk, and outstanding items in the plan of action and milestones.

Primary Responsibility: Information System Owner or Common Control Provider.

Supporting Roles: Authorizing Official or Designated Representative; Information Owner/Steward; Information System Security Officer; Information System Security Engineer; Security Control Assessor.

System Development Life Cycle Phase: Operation/Maintenance.

Supplemental Guidance: The assessment information produced by an assessor during continuous monitoring is provided to the information system owner and common control provider in an updated *security assessment report*. The information system owner and common control provider initiate remediation actions on outstanding items listed in the plan of actions and milestones and findings produced during the ongoing monitoring of security controls. The security control assessor may provide recommendations as to appropriate remediation actions. An assessment of risk (either formal or informal) informs organizational decisions with regard to conducting ongoing remediation actions. Security controls that are modified, enhanced, or added during the continuous monitoring process are reassessed by the assessor to ensure that appropriate corrective actions are taken to eliminate weaknesses or deficiencies or to mitigate the identified risk.

References: NIST Special Publications 800-30, 800-53, 800-53A; CNSS Instruction 1253.

KEY UPDATES

TASK 6-4: Update the security plan, security assessment report, and plan of action and milestones based on the results of the continuous monitoring process.

Primary Responsibility: Information System Owner or Common Control Provider.

Supporting Roles: Information Owner/Steward; Information System Security Officer.

System Development Life Cycle Phase: Operation/Maintenance.

Supplemental Guidance: To facilitate the near real-time management of risk associated with the operation and use of the information system, the organization updates the security plan, security assessment report, and plan of action and milestones on an ongoing basis. The updated security plan reflects any modifications to security controls based on risk mitigation activities carried out by the information system owner or common control provider. The updated security assessment report reflects additional assessment activities carried out to determine security control effectiveness based on modifications to the security plan and deployed controls. The updated plan of action and milestones: (i) reports progress made on the current outstanding items listed in the plan; (ii) addresses vulnerabilities discovered during the security impact analysis or security control monitoring; and (iii) describes how the information system owner or common control provider intends to address those vulnerabilities. The information provided by these key updates helps to raise awareness of the current security state of the information system (and the common controls inherited by the system) thereby supporting the process of ongoing authorization and near real-time risk management.

The frequency of updates to risk management-related information is at the discretion of the information system owner, common control provider, and authorizing officials in accordance with federal and organizational policies. Updates to information regarding the security state of the information system (and common controls inherited by the system) are accurate and timely since the information provided influences ongoing security-related actions and decisions by authorizing officials and other senior leaders within the organization. With the use of automated support tools and effective organization-wide security program management practices, authorizing officials are able to readily access the current security state of the information system including the ongoing effectiveness of system-specific, hybrid, and common controls. This facilitates near real-time management of risk to organizational operations and assets, individuals, other organizations, and the Nation, and provides essential information for continuous monitoring and ongoing authorization.

When updating key information in security plans, security assessment reports, and plans of action and milestones, organizations ensure that the original information needed for oversight, management, and auditing purposes is not modified or destroyed. Providing an effective method of tracking changes to information over time through strict configuration management and control procedures (including version control) is necessary to: (i) achieve transparency in the information security activities of the organization; (ii) obtain individual accountability for security-related actions; and (iii) better understand emerging trends in the organization's information security program.

References: NIST Special Publication 800-53A.

SECURITY STATUS REPORTING

TASK 6-5: Report the security status of the information system (including the effectiveness of security controls employed within and inherited by the system) to the authorizing official and other appropriate organizational officials on an ongoing basis in accordance with the monitoring strategy.

Primary Responsibility: Information System Owner or Common Control Provider.

Supporting Roles: Information System Security Officer.

System Development Life Cycle Phase: Operation/Maintenance.

Supplemental Guidance: The results of monitoring activities are recorded and reported to the authorizing official on an ongoing basis in accordance with the monitoring strategy. Security status reporting can be: (i) event-driven (e.g., when the information system or its environment of operation changes or the system is compromised or breached); (ii) time-driven (e.g., weekly, monthly, quarterly); or (iii) both (event- and time-driven). Security status reports provide the authorizing official and other senior leaders within the organization, essential information with regard to the security state of the information system including the effectiveness of deployed security controls. Security status reports describe the ongoing monitoring activities employed by the information system owner or common control provider. Security status reports also address vulnerabilities in the information system and its environment of operation discovered during the security control assessment, security impact analysis, and security control monitoring and how the information system owner or common control provider intends to address those vulnerabilities.

Organizations have significant latitude and flexibility in the breadth, depth, and formality of security status reports. Security status reports can take whatever form the organization deems most appropriate. The goal is cost-effective and efficient ongoing communication with senior leaders conveying the current security state of the information system and its environment of operation with regard to organizational missions and business functions. At a minimum, security status reports summarize key changes to security plans, security assessment reports, and plans of action and milestones. Use of automated management tools facilitates the effectiveness and timeliness of security status reporting.

The frequency of security status reports is at the discretion of the organization and in accordance with federal and organizational policies. Status reports occur at appropriate intervals to transmit significant security-related information about the information system (including information regarding the ongoing effectiveness of security controls employed within and inherited by the system), but not so frequently as to generate unnecessary work. The authorizing official uses the security status reports in collaboration with the senior information security officer and risk executive (function) to determine if a formal reauthorization action is necessary. Security status reports are appropriately marked, protected, and handled in accordance with federal and organizational policies. At the discretion of the organization, security status reports can be used to help satisfy FISMA reporting requirements for documenting remedial actions for any security-related weaknesses or deficiencies. Note that this status reporting is intended to be ongoing, not to be interpreted as requiring the time, expense, and formality associated with the information provided for the initial approval to operate. Rather, the reporting is conducted in the most cost-effective manner consistent with achieving the reporting objectives.

References: NIST Special Publication 800-53A.

ONGOING RISK DETERMINATION AND ACCEPTANCE

TASK 6-6: Review the reported security status of the information system (including the effectiveness of security controls employed within and inherited by the system) on an ongoing basis in accordance with the monitoring strategy to determine whether the risk to organizational operations, organizational assets, individuals, other organizations, or the Nation remains acceptable.

Primary Responsibility: Authorizing Official.

Supporting Roles: Risk Executive (Function); Authorizing Official Designated Representative; Senior Information Security Officer.

System Development Life Cycle Phase: Operation/Maintenance.

Supplemental Guidance: The authorizing official or designated representative reviews the reported security status of the information system (including the effectiveness of deployed security controls) on an ongoing basis, to determine the current risk to organizational operations and assets, individuals, other organizations, or the Nation. The authorizing official determines, with inputs as appropriate from the authorizing official designated representative, senior information security officer, and the risk executive (function), whether the current risk is acceptable and forwards appropriate direction to the information system owner or common control provider. The use of automated support tools to capture, organize, quantify, visually display, and maintain security status information promotes the concept of *near real-time risk management* regarding the overall risk posture of the organization. The use of metrics and dashboards increases an organization's ability to make risk-based decisions by consolidating data from automated tools and providing it to decision makers at different levels within the organization in an easy-to-understand format. The risks being incurred may change over time based on the information provided in the security status reports. Determining how the changing conditions affect the mission or business risks associated with the information system is essential for maintaining *adequate security*. By carrying out ongoing *risk determination* and *risk acceptance*, authorizing officials can maintain the security authorization over time. Formal reauthorization actions, if required, occur only in accordance with federal or organizational policies. The authorizing official conveys updated risk determination and acceptance results to the risk executive (function).

References: NIST Special Publications 800-30, 800-39.

INFORMATION SYSTEM REMOVAL AND DISPOSAL

TASK 6-7: Implement an information system disposal strategy, when needed, which executes required actions when a system is removed from service.

Primary Responsibility: Information System Owner.

Supporting Roles: Risk Executive (Function); Authorizing Official Designated Representative; Senior Information Security Officer; Information Owner/Steward; Information System Security Officer.

System Development Life Cycle Phase: Disposal.

Supplemental Guidance: When a federal information system is removed from operation, a number of risk management-related actions are required. Organizations ensure that all security controls addressing information system removal and disposal (e.g., media sanitization, configuration management and control) are implemented. Organizational tracking and management systems (including inventory systems) are updated to indicate the specific information system components that are being removed from service. Security status reports reflect the new status of the information system. Users and application owners hosted on the decommissioned information system are notified as appropriate, and any security control inheritance relationships are reviewed and assessed for impact. This task also applies to subsystems that are removed from information systems or decommissioned. The effects of the subsystem removal or disposal are assessed with respect to the overall operation of the information system where the subsystem resided, or in the case of dynamic subsystems, the information systems where the subsystems were actively employed.

References: NIST Special Publications 800-30, 800-53A.

Milestone Checkpoint #6

- Is the organization effectively monitoring changes to the ***information system*** and its ***environment of operation*** including the effectiveness of deployed ***security controls*** in accordance with the continuous monitoring strategy?

- Is the organization effectively analyzing the ***security impacts*** of identified changes to the information system and its environment of operation?

- Is the organization conducting ***ongoing assessments of security controls*** in accordance with the monitoring strategy?

- Is the organization taking the necessary ***remediation actions*** on an ongoing basis to address identified weaknesses and deficiencies in the information system and its environment of operation?

- Does the organization have an effective process in place to report the ***security status*** of the information system and its environment of operation to the authorizing officials and other designated senior leaders within the organization on an ongoing basis?

- Is the organization updating critical ***risk management documents*** based on ongoing monitoring activities?

- Are authorizing officials conducting ***ongoing security authorizations*** by employing effective continuous monitoring activities and communicating updated risk determination and acceptance decisions to information system owners and common control providers?

APPENDIX A

REFERENCES

LAWS, POLICIES, DIRECTIVES, INSTRUCTIONS, STANDARDS, AND GUIDELINES

LEGISLATION

1. E-Government Act [includes FISMA] (P.L. 107-347), December 2002.

2. Federal Information Security Management Act (P.L. 107-347, Title III), December 2002.

3. Paperwork Reduction Act (P.L. 104-13), May 1995.

POLICIES, DIRECTIVES, INSTRUCTIONS

1. Committee on National Security Systems (CNSS) Instruction 4009, *National Information Assurance Glossary*, June 2006.

2. Committee on National Security Systems (CNSS) Instruction 1253, *Security Categorization and Control Selection for National Security Systems*, October 2009.

3. Office of Management and Budget, Circular A-130, Appendix III, Transmittal Memorandum #4, *Management of Federal Information Resources*, November 2000.

4. Office of Management and Budget Memorandum M-02-01, *Guidance for Preparing and Submitting Security Plans of Action and Milestones*, October 2001.

STANDARDS

1. National Institute of Standards and Technology Federal Information Processing Standards Publication 199, *Standards for Security Categorization of Federal Information and Information Systems*, February 2004.

2. National Institute of Standards and Technology Federal Information Processing Standards Publication 200, *Minimum Security Requirements for Federal Information and Information Systems*, March 2006.

GUIDELINES

1. National Institute of Standards and Technology Special Publication 800-18, Revision 1, *Guide for Developing Security Plans for Federal Information Systems*, February 2006.

2. National Institute of Standards and Technology Special Publication 800-27, Revision A, *Engineering Principles for Information Technology Security (A Baseline for Achieving Security)*, June 2004.

3. National Institute of Standards and Technology Special Publication 800-30, *Risk Management Guide for Information Technology Systems*, July 2002.

4. National Institute of Standards and Technology Special Publication 800-39 (Second Public Draft), *Managing Risk from Information Systems: An Organizational Perspective*, April 2008.

5. National Institute of Standards and Technology Special Publication 800-53, Revision 3, *Recommended Security Controls for Federal Information Systems and Organizations*, August 2009.

6. National Institute of Standards and Technology Special Publication 800-53A, *Guide for Assessing the Security Controls in Federal Information Systems: Building Effective Security Assessment Plans*, July 2008.

7. National Institute of Standards and Technology Special Publication 800-59, *Guideline for Identifying an Information System as a National Security System*, August 2003.

8. National Institute of Standards and Technology Special Publication 800-60, Revision 1, *Guide for Mapping Types of Information and Information Systems to Security Categories*, August 2008.

9. National Institute of Standards and Technology Special Publication 800-70, Revision 1, *National Checklist Program for IT Products--Guidelines for Checklist Users and Developers*, September 2009.

10. National Institute of Standards and Technology Special Publication 800-128, *Guide for Security-Focused Configuration Management of Information Systems*, August 2011.

11. National Institute of Standards and Technology Special Publication 800-137, *Information Security Continuous Monitoring for Federal Information Systems and Organizations*, September 2011.

APPENDIX B

GLOSSARY

COMMON TERMS AND DEFINITIONS

Appendix B provides definitions for security terminology used within Special Publication 800-37. Unless specifically defined in this glossary, all terms used in this publication are consistent with the definitions contained in CNSS Instruction 4009, *National Information Assurance Glossary*.

Adequate Security [OMB Circular A-130, Appendix III]	Security commensurate with the risk and the magnitude of harm resulting from the loss, misuse, or unauthorized access to or modification of information. This includes assuring that systems and applications used by the agency operate effectively and provide appropriate confidentiality, integrity, and availability, through the use of cost-effective management, personnel, operational, and technical controls.
Agency	See *Executive Agency*.
Allocation	The process an organization employs to determine whether security controls are defined as system-specific, hybrid, or common. The process an organization employs to assign security controls to specific information system components responsible for providing a particular security capability (e.g., router, server, remote sensor).
Application	A software program hosted by an information system.
Assessment	See *Security Control Assessment*.
Assessor	See *Security Control Assessor*.
Assurance	The grounds for confidence that the set of intended security controls in an information system are effective in their application.
Authorization (to operate)	The official management decision given by a senior organizational official to authorize operation of an information system and to explicitly accept the risk to organizational operations (including mission, functions, image, or reputation), organizational assets, individuals, other organizations, and the Nation based on the implementation of an agreed-upon set of security controls.
Authorization Boundary	All components of an information system to be authorized for operation by an authorizing official and excludes separately authorized systems, to which the information system is connected.
Authorize Processing	See *Authorization*.

Authorizing Official	A senior (federal) official or executive with the authority to formally assume responsibility for operating an information system at an acceptable level of risk to organizational operations (including mission, functions, image, or reputation), organizational assets, individuals, other organizations, and the Nation.
Authorizing Official Designated Representative	An organizational official acting on behalf of an authorizing official in carrying out and coordinating the required activities associated with security authorization.
Availability [44 U.S.C., Sec. 3542]	Ensuring timely and reliable access to and use of information.
Chief Information Officer [PL 104-106, Sec. 5125(b)]	Agency official responsible for: (i) Providing advice and other assistance to the head of the executive agency and other senior management personnel of the agency to ensure that information technology is acquired and information resources are managed in a manner that is consistent with laws, Executive Orders, directives, policies, regulations, and priorities established by the head of the agency; (ii) Developing, maintaining, and facilitating the implementation of a sound and integrated information technology architecture for the agency; and (iii) Promoting the effective and efficient design and operation of all major information resources management processes for the agency, including improvements to work processes of the agency. Note: Organizations subordinate to federal agencies may use the term *Chief Information Officer* to denote individuals filling positions with similar security responsibilities to agency-level Chief Information Officers.
Chief Information Security Officer	See *Senior Agency Information Security Officer*.
Common Control	A security control that is inherited by one or more organizational information systems. See *Security Control Inheritance*.
Common Control Provider	An organizational official responsible for the development, implementation, assessment, and monitoring of common controls (i.e., security controls inherited by information systems).
Compensating Security Controls	The management, operational, and technical controls (i.e., safeguards or countermeasures) employed by an organization in lieu of the recommended controls in the low, moderate, or high baselines described in NIST Special Publication 800-53, that provide equivalent or comparable protection for an information system.
Confidentiality [44 U.S.C., Sec. 3542]	Preserving authorized restrictions on information access and disclosure, including means for protecting personal privacy and proprietary information.

Configuration Control [CNSSI 4009]	Process for controlling modifications to hardware, firmware, software, and documentation to protect the information system against improper modifications before, during, and after system implementation.
Continuous Monitoring	Maintaining ongoing awareness to support organizational risk decisions.
Controlled Interface	A boundary with a set of mechanisms that enforces the security policies and controls the flow of information between interconnected information systems.
Countermeasures [CNSSI 4009]	Actions, devices, procedures, techniques, or other measures that reduce the vulnerability of an information system. Synonymous with security controls and safeguards.
Cross Domain Solution	A form of controlled interface that provides the ability to manually and/or automatically access and/or transfer information between different security domains.
Domain [CNSSI 4009]	An environment or context that includes a set of system resources and a set of system entities that have the right to access the resources as defined by a common security policy, security model, or security architecture. See *Security Domain*.
Dynamic Subsystem	A subsystem that is not continually present during the execution phase of an information system. Service-oriented architectures and cloud computing architectures are examples of architectures that employ dynamic subsystems.
Environment of Operation	The physical surroundings in which an information system processes, stores, and transmits information.
Executive Agency [41 U.S.C., Sec. 403]	An executive department specified in 5 U.S.C., Sec. 101; a military department specified in 5 U.S.C., Sec. 102; an independent establishment as defined in 5 U.S.C., Sec. 104(1); and a wholly owned Government corporation fully subject to the provisions of 31 U.S.C., Chapter 91.
External Information System (or Component)	An information system or component of an information system that is outside of the authorization boundary established by the organization and for which the organization typically has no direct control over the application of required security controls or the assessment of security control effectiveness.
External Information System Service	An information system service that is implemented outside of the authorization boundary of the organizational information system (i.e., a service that is used by, but not a part of, the organizational information system) and for which the organization typically has no direct control over the application of required security controls or the assessment of security control effectiveness.

External Information System Service Provider	A provider of external information system services to an organization through a variety of consumer-producer relationships including but not limited to: joint ventures; business partnerships; outsourcing arrangements (i.e., through contracts, interagency agreements, lines of business arrangements); licensing agreements; and/or supply chain arrangements.
Federal Agency	See *Executive Agency*.
Federal Information System [40 U.S.C., Sec. 11331]	An information system used or operated by an executive agency, by a contractor of an executive agency, or by another organization on behalf of an executive agency.
High-Impact System [FIPS 200]	An information system in which at least one security objective (i.e., confidentiality, integrity, or availability) is assigned a FIPS 199 potential impact value of high.
Hybrid Security Control	A security control that is implemented in an information system in part as a common control and in part as a system-specific control. See *Common Control* and *System-Specific Security Control*.
Information [FIPS 199]	An instance of an information type.
Information Owner [CNSSI 4009]	Official with statutory or operational authority for specified information and responsibility for establishing the controls for its generation, collection, processing, dissemination, and disposal.
Information Resources [44 U.S.C., Sec. 3502]	Information and related resources, such as personnel, equipment, funds, and information technology.
Information Security [44 U.S.C., Sec. 3542]	The protection of information and information systems from unauthorized access, use, disclosure, disruption, modification, or destruction in order to provide confidentiality, integrity, and availability.
Information Security Architect	Individual, group, or organization responsible for ensuring that the information security requirements necessary to protect the organization's core missions and business processes are adequately addressed in all aspects of enterprise architecture including reference models, segment and solution architectures, and the resulting information systems supporting those missions and business processes.
Information Security Policy [CNSSI 4009]	Aggregate of directives, regulations, rules, and practices that prescribes how an organization manages, protects, and distributes information.
Information Security Program Plan	Formal document that provides an overview of the security requirements for an organization-wide information security program and describes the program management controls and common controls in place or planned for meeting those requirements.

Information Steward	Individual or group that helps to ensure the careful and responsible management of federal information belonging to the Nation as a whole, regardless of the entity or source that may have originated, created, or compiled the information. Information stewards provide maximum access to federal information to elements of the federal government and its customers, balanced by the obligation to protect the information in accordance with the provisions of FISMA and any associated security-related federal policies, directives, regulations, standards, and guidance.
Information System [44 U.S.C., Sec. 3502]	A discrete set of information resources organized for the collection, processing, maintenance, use, sharing, dissemination, or disposition of information.
Information System Boundary	See *Authorization Boundary*.
Information System Owner (or Program Manager)	Official responsible for the overall procurement, development, integration, modification, or operation and maintenance of an information system.
Information System Security Engineer	Individual assigned responsibility for conducting information system security engineering activities.
Information System Security Engineering	Process that captures and refines information security requirements and ensures their integration into information technology component products and information systems through purposeful security design or configuration.
Information System-related Security Risks	Information system-related security risks are those risks that arise through the loss of confidentiality, integrity, or availability of information or information systems and consider impacts to the organization (including assets, mission, functions, image, or reputation), individuals, other organizations, and the Nation. See *Risk*.
Information System Security Officer [CNSSI 4009]	Individual with assigned responsibility for maintaining the appropriate operational security posture for an information system or program.

Information Technology [40 U.S.C., Sec. 1401]	Any equipment or interconnected system or subsystem of equipment that is used in the automatic acquisition, storage, manipulation, management, movement, control, display, switching, interchange, transmission, or reception of data or information by the executive agency. For purposes of the preceding sentence, equipment is used by an executive agency if the equipment is used by the executive agency directly or is used by a contractor under a contract with the executive agency which: (i) requires the use of such equipment; or (ii) requires the use, to a significant extent, of such equipment in the performance of a service or the furnishing of a product. The term *information technology* includes computers, ancillary equipment, software, firmware, and similar procedures, services (including support services), and related resources.
Information Type [FIPS 199]	A specific category of information (e.g., privacy, medical, proprietary, financial, investigative, contractor sensitive, security management) defined by an organization or in some instances, by a specific law, Executive Order, directive, policy, or regulation.
Integrity [44 U.S.C., Sec. 3542]	Guarding against improper information modification or destruction, and includes ensuring information non-repudiation and authenticity.
Joint Authorization	Security authorization involving multiple authorizing officials.
Low-Impact System [FIPS 200]	An information system in which all three security objectives (i.e., confidentiality, integrity, and availability) are assigned a FIPS 199 potential impact value of low.
Management Controls [FIPS 200]	The security controls (i.e., safeguards or countermeasures) for an information system that focus on the management of risk and the management of information system security.
Moderate-Impact System [FIPS 200]	An information system in which at least one security objective (i.e., confidentiality, integrity, or availability) is assigned a FIPS 199 potential impact value of moderate, and no security objective is assigned a FIPS 199 potential impact value of high.

National Security System [44 U.S.C., Sec. 3542]	Any information system (including any telecommunications system) used or operated by an agency or by a contractor of an agency, or other organization on behalf of an agency—(i) the function, operation, or use of which involves intelligence activities; involves cryptologic activities related to national security; involves command and control of military forces; involves equipment that is an integral part of a weapon or weapons system; or is critical to the direct fulfillment of military or intelligence missions (excluding a system that is to be used for routine administrative and business applications, for example, payroll, finance, logistics, and personnel management applications); or (ii) is protected at all times by procedures established for information that have been specifically authorized under criteria established by an Executive Order or an Act of Congress to be kept classified in the interest of national defense or foreign policy.
Net-centric Architecture	A complex system of systems composed of subsystems and services that are part of a continuously evolving, complex community of people, devices, information and services interconnected by a network that enhances information sharing and collaboration. Subsystems and services may or may not be developed or owned by the same entity, and, in general, will not be continually present during the full life cycle of the system of systems. Examples of this architecture include service-oriented architectures and cloud computing architectures.
Operational Controls [FIPS 200]	The security controls (i.e., safeguards or countermeasures) for an information system that are primarily implemented and executed by people (as opposed to systems).
Organization [FIPS 200, Adapted]	An entity of any size, complexity, or positioning within an organizational structure (e.g., a federal agency or, as appropriate, any of its operational elements).
Plan of Action and Milestones [OMB Memorandum 02-01]	A document that identifies tasks needing to be accomplished. It details resources required to accomplish the elements of the plan, any milestones in meeting the tasks, and scheduled completion dates for the milestones.
Potential Impact [FIPS 199]	The loss of confidentiality, integrity, or availability could be expected to have: (i) a *limited* adverse effect (FIPS 199 low); (ii) a *serious* adverse effect (FIPS 199 moderate); or (iii) a *severe* or *catastrophic* adverse effect (FIPS 199 high) on organizational operations, organizational assets, or individuals.
Reciprocity	Mutual agreement among participating organizations to accept each other's security assessments in order to reuse information system resources and/or to accept each other's assessed security posture in order to share information.

Risk [FIPS 200, Adapted]	A measure of the extent to which an entity is threatened by a potential circumstance or event, and typically a function of: (i) the adverse impacts that would arise if the circumstance or event occurs; and (ii) the likelihood of occurrence. [Note: Information system-related security risks are those risks that arise from the loss of confidentiality, integrity, or availability of information or information systems and reflect the potential adverse impacts to organizational operations (including mission, functions, image, or reputation), organizational assets, individuals, other organizations, and the Nation. Adverse impacts to the Nation include, for example, compromises to information systems that support critical infrastructure applications or are paramount to government continuity of operations as defined by the Department of Homeland Security.]
Risk Assessment	The process of identifying risks to organizational operations (including mission, functions, image, reputation), organizational assets, individuals, other organizations, and the Nation, resulting from the operation of an information system. Part of risk management, incorporates threat and vulnerability analyses, and considers mitigations provided by security controls planned or in place. Synonymous with risk analysis.
Risk Assessor [NIST SP 800-30]	The individual, group, or organization responsible for conducting a risk assessment.
Risk Executive (Function)	An individual or group within an organization that helps to ensure that: (i) security risk-related considerations for individual information systems, to include the authorization decisions, are viewed from an organization-wide perspective with regard to the overall strategic goals and objectives of the organization in carrying out its missions and business functions; and (ii) managing information system-related security risks is consistent across the organization, reflects organizational risk tolerance, and is considered along with other organizational risks affecting mission/business success.
Risk Management [FIPS 200, Adapted]	The process of managing risks to organizational operations (including mission, functions, image, reputation), organizational assets, individuals, other organizations, and the Nation, resulting from the operation of an information system, and includes: (i) the conduct of a risk assessment; (ii) the implementation of a risk mitigation strategy; and (iii) employment of techniques and procedures for the continuous monitoring of the security state of the information system.
Safeguards [CNSSI 4009]	Protective measures prescribed to meet the security requirements (i.e., confidentiality, integrity, and availability) specified for an information system. Safeguards may include security features, management constraints, personnel security, and security of physical structures, areas, and devices. Synonymous with security controls and countermeasures.
Security Authorization	See *Authorization*.

Security Categorization	The process of determining the security category for information or an information system. Security categorization methodologies are described in CNSS Instruction 1253 for national security systems and in FIPS 199 for other than national security systems.
Security Controls [FIPS 199]	The management, operational, and technical controls (i.e., safeguards or countermeasures) prescribed for an information system to protect the confidentiality, integrity, and availability of the system and its information.
Security Control Assessment	The testing and/or evaluation of the management, operational, and technical security controls in an information system to determine the extent to which the controls are implemented correctly, operating as intended, and producing the desired outcome with respect to meeting the security requirements for the system.
Security Control Assessor	The individual, group, or organization responsible for conducting a security control assessment.
Security Control Inheritance	A situation in which an information system or application receives protection from security controls (or portions of security controls) that are developed, implemented, assessed, authorized, and monitored by entities other than those responsible for the system or application; entities either internal or external to the organization where the system or application resides. See *Common Control*.
Security Domain [CNSSI 4009]	A domain that implements a security policy and is administered by a single authority.
Security Impact Analysis	The analysis conducted by an organizational official to determine the extent to which changes to the information system have affected the security state of the system.
Security Objective [FIPS 199]	Confidentiality, integrity, or availability.
Security Plan	Formal document that provides an overview of the security requirements for an information system or an information security program and describes the security controls in place or planned for meeting those requirements. See *System Security Plan* or *Information Security Program Plan*.
Security Policy [CNSSI 4009]	A set of criteria for the provision of security services.
Security Requirements [FIPS 200]	Requirements levied on an information system that are derived from applicable laws, Executive Orders, directives, policies, standards, instructions, regulations, procedures, or organizational mission/business case needs to ensure the confidentiality, integrity, and availability of the information being processed, stored, or transmitted.

Senior (Agency) Information Security Officer [44 U.S.C., Sec. 3544]	Official responsible for carrying out the Chief Information Officer responsibilities under FISMA and serving as the Chief Information Officer's primary liaison to the agency's authorizing officials, information system owners, and information system security officers. Note: Organizations subordinate to federal agencies may use the term *Senior Information Security Officer* or *Chief Information Security Officer* to denote individuals filling positions with similar responsibilities to Senior Agency Information Security Officers.
Senior Information Security Officer	See *Senior Agency Information Security Officer*.
Subsystem	A major subdivision of an information system consisting of information, information technology, and personnel that performs one or more specific functions.
System	See *Information System*.
System Security Plan [NIST SP 800-18]	Formal document that provides an overview of the security requirements for an information system and describes the security controls in place or planned for meeting those requirements.
System-Specific Security Control	A security control for an information system that has not been designated as a common security control or the portion of a hybrid control that is to be implemented within an information system.
Tailored Security Control Baseline	A set of security controls resulting from the application of tailoring guidance to the security control baseline. See *Tailoring*.
Tailoring	The process by which a security control baseline is modified based on: (i) the application of scoping guidance; (ii) the specification of compensating security controls, if needed; and (iii) the specification of organization-defined parameters in the security controls via explicit assignment and selection statements.
Technical Controls [FIPS 200]	The security controls (i.e., safeguards or countermeasures) for an information system that are primarily implemented and executed by the information system through mechanisms contained in the hardware, software, or firmware components of the system.
Threat [CNSSI 4009, Adapted]	Any circumstance or event with the potential to adversely impact organizational operations (including mission, functions, image, or reputation), organizational assets, individuals, other organizations, or the Nation through an information system via unauthorized access, destruction, disclosure, modification of information, and/or denial of service.
Threat Source [FIPS 200]	The intent and method targeted at the intentional exploitation of a vulnerability or a situation and method that may accidentally trigger a vulnerability. Synonymous with threat agent.
Vulnerability [CNSSI 4009]	Weakness in an information system, system security procedures, internal controls, or implementation that could be exploited or triggered by a threat source.

Vulnerability Assessment
[CNSSI 4009]

Formal description and evaluation of the vulnerabilities in an information system.

ACRONYMS

COMMON ABBREVIATIONS

CIO	Chief Information Officer
CNSS	Committee on National Security Systems
DoD	Department of Defense
FIPS	Federal Information Processing Standards
FISMA	Federal Information Security Management Act
NIST	National Institute of Standards and Technology
NSA	National Security Agency
ODNI	Office of the Director of National Intelligence
OMB	Office of Management and Budget
RMF	Risk Management Framework

ROLES AND RESPONSIBILITIES

KEY PARTICIPANTS IN THE RISK MANAGEMENT PROCESS

The following sections describe the roles and responsibilities of key participants involved in an organization's risk management process.[47] Recognizing that organizations have widely varying missions and organizational structures, there may be differences in naming conventions for risk management-related roles and how specific responsibilities are allocated among organizational personnel (e.g., multiple individuals filling a single role or one individual filling multiple roles).[48] However, the basic functions remain the same. The application of the Risk Management Framework described in this publication is flexible, allowing organizations to effectively accomplish the intent of the specific tasks within their respective organizational structures to best manage information system-related security risks. Many risk management roles defined in this publication have counterpart roles defined in the routine system development life cycle processes carried out by organizations. Whenever possible, organizations align the risk management roles with similar (or complementary) roles defined for the system development life cycle.[49]

D.1 HEAD OF AGENCY (CHIEF EXECUTIVE OFFICER)

The *head of agency* (or chief executive officer) is the highest-level senior official or executive within an organization with the overall responsibility to provide information security protections commensurate with the risk and magnitude of harm (i.e., impact) to organizational operations and assets, individuals, other organizations, and the Nation resulting from unauthorized access, use, disclosure, disruption, modification, or destruction of: (i) information collected or maintained by or on behalf of the agency; and (ii) information systems used or operated by an agency or by a contractor of an agency or other organization on behalf of an agency. Agency heads are also responsible for ensuring that: (i) information security management processes are integrated with strategic and operational planning processes; (ii) senior officials within the organization provide information security for the information and information systems that support the operations and assets under their control; and (iii) the organization has trained personnel sufficient to assist in complying with the information security requirements in related legislation, policies, directives, instructions, standards, and guidelines. Through the development and implementation of strong policies, the head of agency establishes the organizational commitment to information security and the actions required to effectively manage risk and protect the core missions and business functions being carried out by the organization. The head of agency establishes appropriate accountability for information security and provides active support and oversight of monitoring and improvement for the information security program. Senior leadership commitment to information security establishes a level of due diligence within the organization that promotes a climate for mission and business success.

---

[47] Organizations may define other roles (e.g., facilities manager, human resources manager, systems administrator) to support the risk management process.

[48] Caution is exercised when one individual fills multiples roles in the risk management process to ensure that the individual retains an appropriate level of independence and remains free from conflicts of interest.

[49] For example, the system development life cycle role of *system developer* or *program manager* can be aligned with *information system owner*; mission *owner/manager* can be aligned with *authorizing official*; and *system/software engineers* are complementary roles to *information system security engineers*.

D.2 RISK EXECUTIVE (FUNCTION)

The risk executive (function) is an individual or group within an organization that helps to ensure that: (i) risk-related considerations for individual information systems, to include authorization decisions, are viewed from an organization-wide perspective with regard to the overall strategic goals and objectives of the organization in carrying out its core missions and business functions; and (ii) managing information system-related security risks is consistent across the organization, reflects organizational risk tolerance, and is considered along with other types of risks in order to ensure mission/business success. The risk executive (function) coordinates with the senior leadership of an organization to:

- Provide a comprehensive, organization-wide, holistic approach for addressing risk—an approach that provides a greater understanding of the integrated operations of the organization;

- Develop a risk management strategy for the organization providing a strategic view of information security-related risks with regard to the organization as a whole;[50]

- Facilitate the sharing of risk-related information among authorizing officials and other senior leaders within the organization;

- Provide oversight for all risk management-related activities across the organization (e.g., security categorizations) to help ensure consistent and effective risk acceptance decisions;

- Ensure that authorization decisions consider all factors necessary for mission and business success;

- Provide an organization-wide forum to consider all sources of risk (including aggregated risk) to organizational operations and assets, individuals, other organizations, and the Nation;

- Promote cooperation and collaboration among authorizing officials to include authorization actions requiring shared responsibility;

- Ensure that the shared responsibility for supporting organizational mission/business functions using external providers of information and services receives the needed visibility and is elevated to the appropriate decision-making authorities; and

- Identify the organizational risk posture based on the aggregated risk to information from the operation and use of the information systems for which the organization is responsible.

The risk executive (function) presumes neither a specific organizational structure nor formal responsibility assigned to any one individual or group within the organization. The head of the agency/organization may choose to retain the risk executive (function) or to delegate the function to another official or group (e.g., an executive leadership council). The risk executive (function) has inherent U.S. Government authority and is assigned to government personnel only.

D.3 CHIEF INFORMATION OFFICER

The *chief information officer*[51] is an organizational official responsible for: (i) designating a senior information security officer; (ii) developing and maintaining information security policies,

---

[50] Authorizing officials may have narrow or localized perspectives in rendering authorization decisions, in some cases without fully understanding or explicitly accepting the risks being incurred from such decisions.

[51] When an organization has not designated a formal chief information officer position, FISMA requires the associated responsibilities to be handled by a comparable organizational official.

procedures, and control techniques to address all applicable requirements; (iii) overseeing personnel with significant responsibilities for information security and ensuring that the personnel are adequately trained; (iv) assisting senior organizational officials concerning their security responsibilities; and (v) in coordination with other senior officials, reporting annually to the head of the federal agency on the overall effectiveness of the organization's information security program, including progress of remedial actions. The chief information officer, with the support of the risk executive (function) and the senior information security officer, works closely with authorizing officials and their designated representatives to help ensure that:

- An organization-wide information security program is effectively implemented resulting in adequate security for all organizational information systems and environments of operation for those systems;

- Information security considerations are integrated into programming/planning/budgeting cycles, enterprise architectures, and acquisition/system development life cycles;

- Information systems are covered by approved security plans and are authorized to operate;

- Information security-related activities required across the organization are accomplished in an efficient, cost-effective, and timely manner; and

- There is centralized reporting of appropriate information security-related activities.

The chief information officer and authorizing officials also determine, based on organizational priorities, the appropriate allocation of resources dedicated to the protection of the information systems supporting the organization's missions and business functions. For selected information systems, the chief information officer may be designated as an authorizing official or a co-authorizing official with other senior organizational officials. The role of chief information officer has inherent U.S. Government authority and is assigned to government personnel only.

D.4 INFORMATION OWNER/STEWARD

The *information owner/steward* is an organizational official with statutory, management, or operational authority for specified information and the responsibility for establishing the policies and procedures governing its generation, collection, processing, dissemination, and disposal.[52] In information-sharing environments, the information owner/steward is responsible for establishing the rules for appropriate use and protection of the subject information (e.g., rules of behavior) and retains that responsibility even when the information is shared with or provided to other organizations. The owner/steward of the information processed, stored, or transmitted by an information system may or may not be the same as the system owner. A single information system may contain information from multiple information owners/stewards. Information owners/stewards provide input to information system owners regarding the security requirements and security controls for the systems where the information is processed, stored, or transmitted.

---

[52] Federal information is an asset of the Nation, not of a particular federal agency or its subordinate organizations. In that spirit, many federal agencies are developing policies, procedures, processes, and training needed to end the practice of *information ownership* and implement the practice of *information stewardship*. Information stewardship is the careful and responsible management of federal information belonging to the Nation as a whole, regardless of the entity or source that may have originated, created, or compiled the information. Information stewards provide maximum access to federal information to elements of the federal government and its customers, balanced by the obligation to protect the information in accordance with the provisions of FISMA and any associated security-related federal policies, directives, regulations, standards, and guidance.

D.5 SENIOR INFORMATION SECURITY OFFICER

The *senior information security officer* is an organizational official responsible for: (i) carrying out the chief information officer security responsibilities under FISMA; and (ii) serving as the primary liaison for the chief information officer to the organization's authorizing officials, information system owners, common control providers, and information system security officers. The senior information security officer: (i) possesses professional qualifications, including training and experience, required to administer the information security program functions; (ii) maintains information security duties as a primary responsibility; and (iii) heads an office with the mission and resources to assist the organization in achieving more secure information and information systems in accordance with the requirements in FISMA. The senior information security officer (or supporting staff members) may also serve as authorizing official designated representatives or security control assessors. The role of senior information security officer has inherent U.S. Government authority and is assigned to government personnel only.

D.6 AUTHORIZING OFFICIAL

The *authorizing official* is a senior official or executive with the authority to formally assume responsibility for operating an information system at an acceptable level of risk to organizational operations and assets, individuals, other organizations, and the Nation.[53] Authorizing officials typically have budgetary oversight for an information system *or* are responsible for the mission and/or business operations supported by the system. Through the security authorization process, authorizing officials are *accountable* for the security risks associated with information system operations. Accordingly, authorizing officials are in management positions with a level of authority commensurate with understanding and accepting such information system-related security risks. Authorizing officials also approve security plans, memorandums of agreement or understanding, and plans of action and milestones and determine whether significant changes in the information systems or environments of operation require reauthorization. Authorizing officials can deny authorization to operate an information system or if the system is operational, halt operations, if unacceptable risks exist. Authorizing officials coordinate their activities with the risk executive (function), chief information officer, senior information security officer, common control providers, information system owners, information system security officers, security control assessors, and other interested parties during the security authorization process. With the increasing complexity of missions/business processes, partnership arrangements, and the use of external/shared services, it is possible that a particular information system may involve multiple authorizing officials. If so, agreements are established among the authorizing officials and documented in the security plan. Authorizing officials are responsible for ensuring that all activities and functions associated with security authorization that are delegated to authorizing official designated representatives are carried out. The role of authorizing official has inherent U.S. Government authority and is assigned to government personnel only.

D.7 AUTHORIZING OFFICIAL DESIGNATED REPRESENTATIVE

The *authorizing official designated representative* is an organizational official that acts on behalf of an authorizing official to coordinate and conduct the required day-to-day activities associated with the security authorization process. Authorizing official designated representatives can be empowered by authorizing officials to make certain decisions with regard to the planning and resourcing of the security authorization process, approval of the security plan, approval and monitoring the implementation of plans of action and milestones, and the assessment and/or

---

[53] The responsibility of authorizing officials described in FIPS 200, was extended in NIST Special Publication 800-53 to include risks to other organizations and the Nation.

determination of risk. The designated representative may also be called upon to prepare the final authorization package, obtain the authorizing official's signature on the authorization decision document, and transmit the authorization package to appropriate organizational officials. The only activity that cannot be delegated to the designated representative by the authorizing official is the authorization decision and signing of the associated authorization decision document (i.e., the acceptance of risk to organizational operations and assets, individuals, other organizations, and the Nation).

D.8 COMMON CONTROL PROVIDER

The *common control provider* is an individual, group, or organization responsible for the development, implementation, assessment, and monitoring of common controls (i.e., security controls inherited by information systems).[54] Common control providers are responsible for: (i) documenting the organization-identified common controls in a *security plan* (or equivalent document prescribed by the organization); (ii) ensuring that required assessments of common controls are carried out by qualified assessors with an appropriate level of independence defined by the organization; (iii) documenting assessment findings in a *security assessment report*; and (iv) producing a *plan of action and milestones* for all controls having weaknesses or deficiencies. Security plans, security assessment reports, and plans of action and milestones for common controls (or a summary of such information) is made available to information system owners *inheriting* those controls after the information is reviewed and approved by the senior official or executive with oversight responsibility for those controls.

D.9 INFORMATION SYSTEM OWNER

The *information system owner* is an organizational official responsible for the procurement, development, integration, modification, operation, maintenance, and disposal of an information system.[55] The information system owner is responsible for addressing the operational interests of the user community (i.e., users who require access to the information system to satisfy mission, business, or operational requirements) and for ensuring compliance with information security requirements. In coordination with the information system security officer, the information system owner is responsible for the development and maintenance of the security plan and ensures that the system is deployed and operated in accordance with the agreed-upon security controls. In coordination with the information owner/steward, the information system owner is also responsible for deciding who has access to the system (and with what types of privileges or access rights)[56] and ensures that system users and support personnel receive the requisite security training (e.g., instruction in rules of behavior). Based on guidance from the authorizing official, the information system owner informs appropriate organizational officials of the need to conduct the security authorization, ensures that the necessary resources are available for the effort, and provides the required information system access, information, and documentation to the security

---

[54] Organizations can have multiple common control providers depending on how information security responsibilities are allocated organization-wide. Common control providers may also be *information system owners* when the common controls are resident within an information system. Common controls are described in Section 2.4.

[55] The *information system owner* serves as the focal point for the information system. In that capacity, the information system owner serves both as an owner and as the central point of contact between the authorization process and the owners of components of the system including, for example: (i) applications, networking, servers, or workstations; (ii) owners/stewards of information processed, stored, or transmitted by the system; and (iii) owners of the missions and business functions supported by the system. Some organizations may refer to information system owners as program managers or business/asset owners.

[56] The responsibility for deciding who has access to specific information within an information system (and with what types of privileges or access rights) may reside with the information owner/steward.

control assessor. The information system owner receives the security assessment results from the security control assessor. After taking appropriate steps to reduce or eliminate vulnerabilities, the information system owner assembles the authorization package and submits the package to the authorizing official or the authorizing official designated representative for adjudication.[57]

D.10 INFORMATION SYSTEM SECURITY OFFICER

The *information system security officer*[58] is an individual responsible for ensuring that the appropriate operational security posture is maintained for an information system and as such, works in close collaboration with the information system owner. The information system security officer also serves as a principal advisor on all matters, technical and otherwise, involving the security of an information system. The information system security officer has the detailed knowledge and expertise required to manage the security aspects of an information system and, in many organizations, is assigned responsibility for the day-to-day security operations of a system. This responsibility may also include, but is not limited to, physical and environmental protection, personnel security, incident handling, and security training and awareness. The information system security officer may be called upon to assist in the development of the security policies and procedures and to ensure compliance with those policies and procedures. In close coordination with the information system owner, the information system security officer often plays an active role in the monitoring of a system and its environment of operation to include developing and updating the security plan, managing and controlling changes to the system, and assessing the security impact of those changes.

D.11 INFORMATION SECURITY ARCHITECT

The *information security architect* is an individual, group, or organization responsible for ensuring that the information security requirements necessary to protect the organization's core missions and business processes are adequately addressed in all aspects of enterprise architecture including reference models, segment and solution architectures, and the resulting information systems supporting those missions and business processes. The information security architect serves as the liaison between the enterprise architect and the information system security engineer and also coordinates with information system owners, common control providers, and information system security officers on the allocation of security controls as system-specific, hybrid, or common controls. In addition, information security architects, in close coordination with information system security officers, advise authorizing officials, chief information officers, senior information security officers, and the risk executive (function), on a range of security-related issues including, for example, establishing information system boundaries, assessing the severity of weaknesses and deficiencies in the information system, plans of action and milestones, risk mitigation approaches, security alerts, and potential adverse effects of identified vulnerabilities.

---

[57] Depending on how the organization has organized its security authorization activities, the authorizing official may choose to designate an individual other than the information system owner to compile and assemble the information for the security authorization package. In this situation, the designated individual must coordinate the compilation and assembly activities with the information system owner.

[58] Organizations may also define an *information system security manager* or *information security manager* role with similar responsibilities as an information system security officer or with oversight responsibilities for an information security program. In these situations, information system security officers may, at the discretion of the organization, report directly to information system security managers or information security managers.

D.12 INFORMATION SYSTEM SECURITY ENGINEER

The *information system security engineer* is an individual, group, or organization responsible for conducting information system security engineering activities. Information system security engineering is a process that captures and refines information security requirements and ensures that the requirements are effectively integrated into information technology component products and information systems through purposeful security architecting, design, development, and configuration. Information system security engineers are an integral part of the development team (e.g., integrated project team) designing and developing organizational information systems or upgrading legacy systems. Information system security engineers employ best practices when implementing security controls within an information system including software engineering methodologies, system/security engineering principles, secure design, secure architecture, and secure coding techniques. System security engineers coordinate their security-related activities with information security architects, senior information security officers, information system owners, common control providers, and information system security officers.

D.13 SECURITY CONTROL ASSESSOR

The *security control assessor*[59] is an individual, group, or organization responsible for conducting a comprehensive assessment of the management, operational, and technical security controls and control enhancements employed within or inherited by an information system to determine the overall effectiveness of the controls (i.e., the extent to which the controls are implemented correctly, operating as intended, and producing the desired outcome with respect to meeting the security requirements for the system). Security control assessors also provide an assessment of the severity of weaknesses or deficiencies discovered in the information system and its environment of operation and recommend corrective actions to address identified vulnerabilities. In addition to the above responsibilities, security control assessors prepare the final security assessment report containing the results and findings from the assessment. Prior to initiating the security control assessment, an assessor conducts an assessment of the security plan to help ensure that the plan provides a set of security controls for the information system that meet the stated security requirements.

The required level of assessor independence is determined by the specific conditions of the security control assessment. For example, when the assessment is conducted in support of an authorization decision or ongoing authorization, the authorizing official makes an explicit determination of the degree of independence required in accordance with federal policies, directives, standards, and guidelines. Assessor independence is an important factor in: (i) preserving the impartial and unbiased nature of the assessment process; (ii) determining the credibility of the security assessment results; and (iii) ensuring that the authorizing official receives the most objective information possible in order to make an informed, risk-based, authorization decision. The information system owner and common control provider rely on the security expertise and the technical judgment of the assessor to: (i) assess the security controls employed within and inherited by the information system using assessment procedures specified in the security assessment plan; and (ii) provide specific recommendations on how to correct weaknesses or deficiencies in the controls and address identified vulnerabilities.

---

[59] Security control assessors may be called *certification agents* in some organizations. At the discretion of the organization, security control assessors may be given additional duties/responsibilities for the post processing and analysis of security control assessment findings and results. This may include, for example, making specific determinations for or recommendations to authorizing officials (known in some communities of interest as *certification recommendations* or *certification determinations*).

SUMMARY OF RMF TASKS

LISTING OF PRIMARY RESPONSIBILITIES AND SUPPORTING ROLES

RMF TASKS	PRIMARY RESPONSIBILITY	SUPPORTING ROLES
RMF Step 1: Categorize Information System		
TASK 1-1 **Security Categorization** Categorize the information system and document the results of the security categorization in the security plan.	Information System Owner Information Owner/Steward	Risk Executive (Function) Authorizing Official *or* Designated Representative Chief Information Officer Senior Information Security Officer Information System Security Officer
TASK 1-2 **Information System Description** Describe the information system (including system boundary) and document the description in the security plan.	Information System Owner	Authorizing Official *or* Designated Representative Senior Information Security Officer Information Owner/Steward Information System Security Officer
TASK 1-3 **Information System Registration** Register the information system with appropriate organizational program/management offices.	Information System Owner	Information System Security Officer
RMF Step 2: Select Security Controls		
TASK 2-1 **Common Control Identification** Identify the security controls that are provided by the organization as common controls for organizational information systems and document the controls in a security plan (or equivalent document).	Chief Information Officer *or* Senior Information Security Officer Information Security Architect Common Control Provider	Risk Executive (Function) Authorizing Official *or* Designated Representative Information System Owner Information System Security Engineer
TASK 2-2 **Security Control Selection** Select the security controls for the information system and document the controls in the security plan.	Information Security Architect Information System Owner	Authorizing Official *or* Designated Representative Information Owner/Steward Information System Security Officer Information System Security Engineer

RMF TASKS	PRIMARY RESPONSIBILITY	SUPPORTING ROLES
TASK 2-3 **Monitoring Strategy** Develop a strategy for the continuous monitoring of security control effectiveness and any proposed/actual changes to the information system and its environment of operation.	Information System Owner *or* Common Control Provider	Risk Executive (Function) Authorizing Official *or* Designated Representative Chief Information Officer Senior Information Security Officer Information Owner/Steward Information System Security Officer
TASK 2-4 **Security Plan Approval** Review and approve the security plan.	Authorizing Official *or* Designated Representative	Risk Executive (Function) Chief Information Officer Senior Information Security Officer
RMF Step 3: Implement Security Controls		
TASK 3-1 **Security Control Implementation** Implement the security controls specified in the security plan.	Information System Owner *or* Common Control Provider	Information Owner/Steward Information System Security Officer Information System Security Engineer
TASK 3-2 **Security Control Documentation** Document the security control implementation, as appropriate, in the security plan, providing a functional description of the control implementation (including planned inputs, expected behavior, and expected outputs).	Information System Owner *or* Common Control Provider	Information Owner/Steward Information System Security Officer Information System Security Engineer
RMF Step 4: Assess Security Controls		
TASK 4-1 **Assessment Preparation** Develop, review, and approve a plan to assess the security controls.	Security Control Assessor	Authorizing Official *or* Designated Representative Chief Information Officer Senior Information Security Officer Information System Owner *or* Common Control Provider Information Owner/Steward Information System Security Officer
TASK 4-2 **Security Control Assessment** Assess the security controls in accordance with the assessment procedures defined in the security assessment plan.	Security Control Assessor	Information System Owner *or* Common Control Provider Information Owner/Steward Information System Security Officer

RMF TASKS	PRIMARY RESPONSIBILITY	SUPPORTING ROLES
TASK 4-3 **Security Assessment Report** Prepare the security assessment report documenting the issues, findings, and recommendations from the security control assessment.	Security Control Assessor	Information System Owner *or* Common Control Provider Information System Security Officer
TASK 4-4 **Remediation Actions** Conduct initial remediation actions on security controls based on the findings and recommendations of the security assessment report and reassess remediated control(s), as appropriate.	Information System Owner *or* Common Control Provider Security Control Assessor	Authorizing Official *or* Designated Representative Chief Information Officer Senior Information Security Officer Information Owner/Steward Information System Security Officer Information System Security Engineer
RMF Step 5: Authorize Information System		
TASK 5-1 **Plan of Action and Milestones** Prepare the plan of action and milestones based on the findings and recommendations of the security assessment report excluding any remediation actions taken.	Information System Owner *or* Common Control Provider	Information Owner/Steward Information System Security Officer
TASK 5-2 **Security Authorization Package** Assemble the security authorization package and submit the package to the authorizing official for adjudication.	Information System Owner *or* Common Control Provider	Information System Security Officer Security Control Assessor
TASK 5-3 **Risk Determination** Determine the risk to organizational operations (including mission, functions, image, or reputation), organizational assets, individuals, other organizations, or the Nation.	Authorizing Official *or* Designated Representative	Risk Executive (Function) Senior Information Security Officer
TASK 5-4 **Risk Acceptance** Determine if the risk to organizational operations, organizational assets, individuals, other organizations, or the Nation is acceptable.	Authorizing Official	Risk Executive (Function) Authorizing Official Designated Representative Senior Information Security Officer

RMF TASKS	PRIMARY RESPONSIBILITY	SUPPORTING ROLES
RMF Step 6: Monitor Security Controls		
TASK 6-1 **Information System and Environment Changes** Determine the security impact of proposed or actual changes to the information system and its environment of operation.	Information System Owner *or* Common Control Provider	Risk Executive (Function) Authorizing Official *or* Designated Representative Senior Information Security Officer Information Owner/Steward Information System Security Officer
TASK 6-2 **Ongoing Security Control Assessments** Assess the technical, management, and operational security controls employed within and inherited by the information system in accordance with the organization-defined monitoring strategy.	Security Control Assessor	Authorizing Official *or* Designated Representative Information System Owner *or* Common Control Provider Information Owner/Steward Information System Security Officer
TASK 6-3 **Ongoing Remediation Actions** Conduct remediation actions based on the results of ongoing monitoring activities, assessment of risk, and outstanding items in the plan of action and milestones.	Information System Owner *or* Common Control Provider	Authorizing Official *or* Designated Representative Information Owner/Steward Information System Security Officer Information System Security Engineer Security Control Assessor
TASK 6-4 **Key Updates** Update the security plan, security assessment report, and plan of action and milestones based on the results of the continuous monitoring process.	Information System Owner *or* Common Control Provider	Information Owner/Steward Information System Security Officer
TASK 6-5 **Security Status Reporting** Report the security status of the information system (including the effectiveness of security controls employed within and inherited by the system) to the authorizing official and other appropriate organizational officials on an ongoing basis in accordance with the monitoring strategy.	Information System Owner *or* Common Control Provider	Information System Security Officer

RMF TASKS	PRIMARY RESPONSIBILITY	SUPPORTING ROLES
TASK 6-6 **Ongoing Risk Determination and Acceptance** Review the reported security status of the information system (including the effectiveness of security controls employed within and inherited by the system) on an ongoing basis in accordance with the monitoring strategy to determine whether the risk to organizational operations, organizational assets, individuals, other organizations, or the Nation remains acceptable.	Authorizing Official	Risk Executive (Function) Authorizing Official Designated Representative Senior Information Security Officer
TASK 6-7 **Information System Removal and Disposal** Implement an information system disposal strategy, when needed, which executes required actions when a system is removed from service.	Information System Owner	Risk Executive (Function) Authorizing Official Designated Representative Senior Information Security Officer Information Owner/Steward Information System Security Officer

APPENDIX F

SECURITY AUTHORIZATION

AUTHORIZATION DECISIONS AND SUPPORTING EVIDENCE

This appendix provides information on the security authorization process to include: (i) the content of the authorization package; (ii) types of authorization decisions; (iii) the content of the authorization decision document; and (iv) maintenance of authorizations through continuous monitoring processes and conditions for reauthorization.

F.1 AUTHORIZATION PACKAGE

The security *authorization package* documents the results of the security control assessment and provides the authorizing official with essential information needed to make a risk-based decision on whether to authorize operation of an information system or a designated set of common controls. Unless specifically designated otherwise by the chief information officer or authorizing official, the information system owner or common control provider is responsible for the assembly, compilation, and submission of the authorization package. The information system owner or common control provider receives inputs from the information system security officer, security control assessor, senior information security officer, and risk executive (function) during the preparation of the authorization package. The authorization package[60] contains the following documents:

- Security plan;
- Security assessment report; and
- Plan of action and milestones.

The *security plan*, prepared by the information system owner or common control provider, provides an overview of the security requirements and describes the security controls in place or planned for meeting those requirements. The plan provides sufficient information to understand the intended or actual implementation of each security control employed within or inherited by the information system.[61] The security plan also contains as supporting appendices or as references to appropriate sources, other risk and security-related documents such as a risk assessment, privacy impact assessment, system interconnection agreements, contingency plan, security configurations, configuration management plan, incident response plan, and continuous monitoring strategy. In accordance with the *near real-time* risk management objectives of the security authorization process, the security plan is updated whenever events dictate changes to the security controls employed within or inherited by the information system. Updates to the security plan may be triggered by a variety of events, including for example: (i) a vulnerability scan of the information system or vulnerability assessment of the environment of operation; (ii) new threat information; (iii) weaknesses or deficiencies discovered in currently deployed security controls

---

[60] The authorizing official determines what additional supporting documentation or references may be required to be included in the security authorization package. Appropriate measures are employed to protect information contained in security authorization packages in accordance with federal and organizational policy.

[61] The *security plan* is a conceptual body of information which may be accounted for within one or more repositories and include documents (electronic or hard copy) that come from a variety of sources produced throughout the system development life cycle. For example, information system owners inheriting common controls can either document the implementation of the controls in their respective security plans or reference the controls contained in the security plans of common control providers.

after an information system breach; (iv) a redefinition of mission priorities or business objectives invalidating the results of the previous security categorization process; and (v) a change in the information system (e.g., adding new hardware, software, or firmware; establishing new connections) or its environment of operation (e.g., moving to a new facility).

The *security assessment report*, prepared by the security control assessor, provides the results of assessing the implementation of the security controls identified in the security plan to determine the extent to which the controls are implemented correctly, operating as intended, and producing the desired outcome with respect to meeting the specified security requirements. The security assessment report also contains a list of recommended corrective actions for any weaknesses or deficiencies identified in the security controls.[62] Supporting the near real-time risk management objectives of the security authorization process, the security assessment report is updated on an ongoing basis whenever changes are made to the security controls employed within or inherited by the information system.[63] Updates to the security assessment report help to ensure that the information system owner, common control provider, and authorizing officials maintain the appropriate awareness with regard to security control effectiveness. The overall effectiveness of the security controls directly affects the ultimate security state of the information system and decisions regarding explicit acceptance of risk.

The *plan of action and milestones*, prepared by the information system owner or common control provider, describes the specific measures planned: (i) to correct weaknesses or deficiencies noted in the security controls during the assessment; and (ii) to address known vulnerabilities in the information system.[64] The content and structure of plans of action and milestones are informed by the organizational risk management strategy developed as part of the risk executive (function) and is consistent with the plans of action and milestones process established by the organization and any specific requirements defined in federal policies, directives, memoranda, or regulations. The most effective plans of action and milestones contain a robust set of actual weaknesses or deficiencies identified in the security controls employed within or inherited by the information system. Assuming that most information systems and the environments in which those systems are deployed, have more vulnerabilities than available resources can realistically address, organizations define a strategy for developing and implementing plans of action and milestones that facilitates a prioritized approach to risk mitigation and that is consistent across the organization. This strategy helps to ensure that plans of action and milestones are based on:

- The security categorization of the information system;

- The specific weaknesses or deficiencies in the security controls;

- The importance of the identified security control weaknesses or deficiencies (i.e., the direct or indirect effect the weaknesses or deficiencies may have on the overall security state of the information system and hence on the risk exposure[65] of the organization);

---

[62] Organizations may choose to develop an *executive summary* from the detailed findings that are generated during a security control assessment. An executive summary provides an authorizing official with an abbreviated version of the security assessment report focusing on the highlights of the assessment, synopsis of key findings, and recommendations for addressing weaknesses and deficiencies in the security controls.

[63] Organizations maintain strict version control as critical documents in the authorization package are updated.

[64] Organizations may choose to document the specific measures *implemented* to correct weaknesses or deficiencies in security controls in the plan of action and milestones, thereby providing an historical record of actions completed.

[65] In general, risk exposure is the degree to which an organization is threatened by the potential adverse effects on organizational operations and assets, individuals, other organizations, or the Nation.

- The organization's proposed risk mitigation approach to address the identified weaknesses or deficiencies in the security controls (e.g., prioritization of risk mitigation actions, allocation of risk mitigation resources); and

- The organization's rationale for accepting certain weaknesses or deficiencies in the security controls.[66]

Organizational strategies for plans of action and milestones are guided by the security categories of the respective information systems affected by the risk mitigation activities. Organizations may decide, for example, to allocate the vast majority of risk mitigation resources initially to the *highest-impact* information systems because a failure to correct the weaknesses or deficiencies in those systems could potentially have the most significant adverse effects on the organization's missions or business operations. Organizations also prioritize weaknesses or deficiencies using information from organizational assessments of risk and the risk management strategy developed as part of the risk executive (function). Therefore, a high-impact system would have a prioritized list of weaknesses or deficiencies for that system, as would moderate-impact and low-impact systems. In general, the plan of action and milestones strategy always addresses the highest-priority weaknesses or deficiencies within those prioritized systems.

After completion of the security plan, security assessment report, and plan of action and milestones, the information system owner or common control provider submits the final security authorization package to the authorizing official or designated representative. Figure F-1 illustrates the key sections of the authorization package.

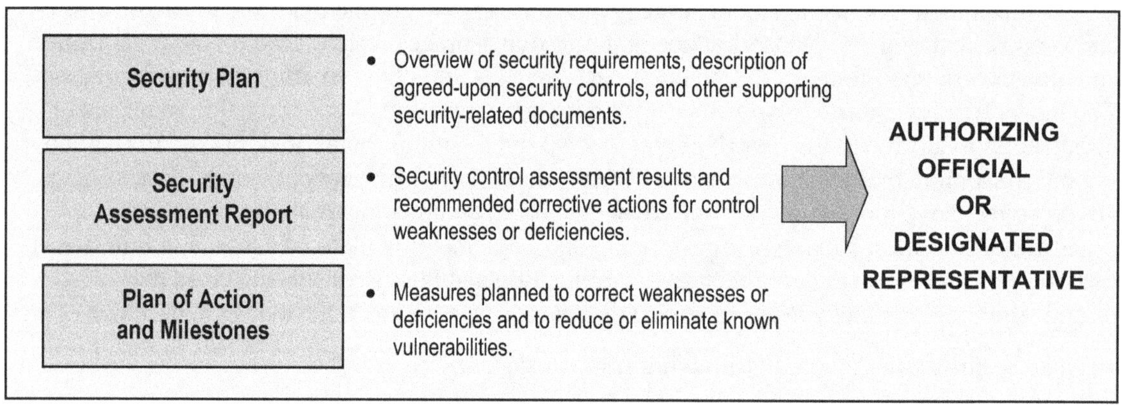

FIGURE F-1: SECURITY AUTHORIZATION PACKAGE

F.2 AUTHORIZATION DECISIONS

Authorization decisions are based on the content of the authorization package including inputs from the organization's risk executive (function) and any additional supporting documentation required by the authorizing official. The security authorization package provides comprehensive information on the security state of the information system. Risk executive (function) inputs, including the previously established overarching risk guidance derived from the risk management strategy, provide additional information to the authorizing official that may be relevant and affect the final authorization decision (e.g., organizational risk tolerance, organization's overall risk mitigation strategy, core mission and business requirements, dependencies among information systems, ongoing risk monitoring requirements, and other types of risks not directly associated

---

[66] Organizations document their rationale for accepting security control weakness or deficiencies.

with the information system or its environment of operation). Risk executive (function) inputs are documented and become part of the authorization decision. Organizations determine how the risk management strategy and risk-related guidance from the risk executive (function) influences/impacts the authorization decisions of authorizing officials. Security authorization decisions are conveyed to information system owners and common control providers and are made available to selected officials within the organization (e.g., information system owners inheriting common controls, authorizing officials for interconnected systems, chief information officers, senior information security officers, information owners/stewards). There are two types of authorization decisions that can be rendered by authorizing officials:

- Authorization to operate;[67] and

- Denial of authorization to operate.

Authorization to Operate

If the authorizing official, after reviewing the authorization package and any additional inputs provided by the risk executive (function), deems that the risk to organizational operations and assets, individuals, other organizations, and the Nation is acceptable, an *authorization to operate* is issued for the information system or for the common controls inherited by organizational information systems. The information system is authorized to operate for a specified time period in accordance with the terms and conditions established by the authorizing official.[68] For common control providers external to an information system, the authorization decision means that the common controls under their control are approved for *inheritance* by organizational information systems. An *authorization termination date* is also established by the authorizing official as a condition of authorization. The authorization termination date can be adjusted by the authorizing official to reflect an increased level of concern regarding the security state of the information system including the security control employed within or inherited by the system. Authorization termination dates do not exceed the maximum allowable time periods for authorization established by federal or organizational policy.

The authorizing official takes specific actions to reduce or eliminate vulnerabilities identified during the execution of the Risk Management Framework unless the vulnerabilities have been explicitly accepted as part of the authorization decision. In addition, the information system owner or common control provider establishes a disciplined, structured, and repeatable process to monitor the ongoing effectiveness of the deployed security controls and the progress of any actions taken to correct or eliminate weaknesses or deficiencies. The plan of action and milestones submitted by the information system owner is used by the authorizing official to monitor the progress in correcting deficiencies and weaknesses noted during the security control assessment.

---

[67] An *interim authorization to test* is a special type of authorization decision allowing an information system to operate in an operational environment for the express purpose of testing the system with actual operational (i.e., live) data for a specified time period. An interim authorization to test is granted by an authorizing official only when the operational environment or live data is required to complete specific test objectives.

[68] Some organizations may choose to use the term *interim authorization to operate* to focus attention on the increased risk being accepted by the authorizing official in situations where there are significant weaknesses or deficiencies in the information system, but an overarching mission necessity requires placing the system into operation or continuing its operation.

Denial of Authorization to Operate

If the authorizing official, after reviewing the authorization package and any additional inputs provided by the risk executive (function), deems that the risk to organizational operations and assets, individuals, other organizations, and the Nation is unacceptable and immediate steps cannot be taken to reduce the risk to an acceptable level, a *denial of authorization to operate* is issued for the information system or for the common controls inherited by organizational information systems. The information system is not authorized to operate and is not placed into operation. If the system is currently in operation, all activity is halted. For common control providers external to an information system, the authorization decision means that the common controls under their control are *not* approved for *inheritance* by organizational information systems. Failure to receive an authorization to operate indicates that there are major weaknesses or deficiencies in the security controls employed within or inherited by the information system. The authorizing official or designated representative works with the information system owner or common control provider to revise the plan of action and milestones to ensure that appropriate measures are taken to correct the identified weaknesses or deficiencies.

A special case of a denial of authorization to operate is an *authorization rescission*. Authorizing officials can rescind a previous authorization decision at any time in situations where there is a specific violation of: (i) federal/organizational security policies, directives, regulations, standards, guidance, or practices; or (ii) the terms and conditions of the original authorization. For example, failure to maintain an effective continuous monitoring program may be grounds for rescinding an authorization decision. Authorizing officials consult with the risk executive (function) and the senior information security officer before rescinding security authorizations.

F.3 AUTHORIZATION DECISION DOCUMENT

The *authorization decision document* transmits the final security authorization decision from the authorizing official to the information system owner or common control provider and other key organizational officials, as appropriate. The authorization decision document contains the following information:

- Authorization decision;
- Terms and conditions for the authorization;
- Authorization termination date; and
- Risk executive (function) input (if provided).

The security *authorization decision* indicates whether the information system is: (i) authorized to operate; or (ii) not authorized to operate. For common controls, the authorization decision means that the controls are approved for *inheritance* by organizational information systems. The *terms and conditions* for the authorization provide a description of any limitations or restrictions placed on the operation of the information system or the implementation of common controls that must be followed by the system owner or common control provider. The *authorization termination date*, established by the authorizing official, indicates when the security authorization expires and reauthorization is required. An authorizing official designated representative prepares the authorization decision document for the authorizing official with authorization recommendations, as appropriate. The authorization decision document is attached to the original authorization package and transmitted to the information system owner or common control provider.[69]

---

[69] Authorization decision documents may be digitally signed to ensure authenticity.

Upon receipt of the authorization decision document and authorization package, the information system owner or common control provider acknowledges and implements the terms and conditions of the authorization and notifies the authorizing official. The information system owner or common control provider retains the original authorization decision document and authorization package.[70] The organization ensures that authorization documents for information systems and for common controls are available to appropriate organizational officials (e.g., information system owners inheriting common controls, the risk executive [function], chief information officers, senior information security officers, information system security officers). The contents of the security authorization documentation, especially information regarding information system vulnerabilities, are: (i) marked and appropriately protected in accordance with federal/organizational policy; and (ii) retained in accordance with the organization's record retention policy. The authorizing official verifies on an ongoing basis, that the terms and conditions established as part of the authorization are being followed by the information system owner or common control provider.

F.4 ONGOING AUTHORIZATION

A robust and comprehensive continuous monitoring[71] strategy integrated into the organization's system development life cycle process, promotes risk management on an ongoing basis and can significantly reduce the resources required for reauthorization, if required. Using automation and state-of-the-practice tools, techniques, and procedures, risk management can become *near real-time* with ongoing monitoring of security controls and changes to the information system and its environment of operation. When monitoring is conducted in accordance with the needs of the authorizing official, that monitoring results in the production of key information needed to determine: (i) the current security state of the information system (including the effectiveness of the security controls employed within and inherited by the system); (ii) the resulting risks to organizational operations, organizational assets, individuals, other organizations, and the Nation; and (iii) whether to authorize continued operation of the system or continued use of common controls inherited by organizational information systems. Organizations provide an official designation (including any approvals required) for information systems that have transitioned from initial authorization to operate into an ongoing authorization approach.

Continuous monitoring also helps to amortize the resource expenditures for reauthorization activities over the authorization period. The ultimate objective is to achieve a state of *ongoing authorization* where the authorizing official maintains sufficient knowledge of the current security state of the information system (including the effectiveness of the security controls employed within and inherited by the system) to determine whether continued operation is acceptable based on ongoing risk determinations, and if not, which step or steps in the Risk Management Framework needs to be re-executed in order to effectively respond to the additional risk. Formal reauthorization actions are avoided in situations where the continuous monitoring process provides authorizing officials the necessary information to manage the potential risk arising from changes to the information system or its environment of operation. Organizations maximize the use of status reports and security state information produced during the continuous monitoring process to minimize the level of effort required if a formal reauthorization action is required.

---

[70] Organizations may choose to employ automated tools to support the development, distribution, and archiving of risk management documentation to include artifacts associated with the security authorization process.

[71] Continuous monitoring is described in Appendix G. NIST Special Publication 800-137 provides additional guidance for Information Security Continuous Monitoring Programs.

When an information system is under ongoing authorization, the system may be authorized for ongoing operation on a *time-driven* or *event-driven* basis, leveraging the security-related information generated by the continuous monitoring program. The system is reviewed and authorized for ongoing operation on a time-driven basis in accordance with the authorization frequency determined as part of the continuous monitoring strategy. The system is reviewed and authorized for ongoing operation on an event-driven basis when pre-defined (trigger) events occur or at the discretion of the authorizing official. Whether the authorization for ongoing operation is time-driven or event-driven, the authorizing official acknowledges ongoing acceptance of identified risks. The organization determines the level of formality required for such acknowledgement by the authorizing official.

F.5 REAUTHORIZATION

Formal reauthorization actions occur at the discretion of the authorizing official in accordance with federal or organizational policy. If a formal reauthorization action is required, organizations maximize the use of security and risk-related information produced as part of the continuous monitoring processes currently in effect. Formal reauthorization actions, if initiated, can be either *time-driven* or *event-driven*. Time-driven reauthorizations occur when the authorization termination date is reached (if one is specified). If the information system is under ongoing authorization (i.e., a continuous monitoring program is in place that monitors all implemented common, hybrid, and system-specific controls with the frequency specified in the continuous monitoring strategy), time-driven reauthorizations may not be necessary. However, if the continuous monitoring program is not yet comprehensive enough to fully support ongoing authorization, a maximum authorization period can be specified by the authorizing official. Authorization termination dates are influenced by federal and/or organizational policies and by the requirements of authorizing officials which may establish maximum authorization periods.

For security control assessments associated with reauthorization, organizations leverage security-related information generated by the existing continuous monitoring program and fill in any gaps with manual or procedural assessments. Organizations may also supplement automatically-generated information with manually/procedurally-generated assessment information in situations where greater assurance is needed. If the security control assessments are conducted by qualified assessors with the required degree of *independence* based on federal/organizational policies, appropriate security standards and guidelines, and the needs of the authorizing official, the assessment results can be cumulatively applied to the reauthorization.[72] The reauthorization action can be as simple as updating the security status information in the authorization package (i.e., the security plan, security assessment report, and plan of action and milestones). The authorizing official subsequently signs an updated authorization decision document based on the current determination and acceptance of risk to organizational operations and assets, individuals, other organizations, and the Nation.[73]

In the event that there is a change in authorizing officials, the new authorizing official reviews the current authorization decision document, authorization package, and any updated documents created as a result of the ongoing monitoring activities. If the new authorizing official is willing to accept the currently documented risk, then the official signs a new authorization decision document, thus formally transferring responsibility and accountability for the information system

---

[72] NIST Special Publication 800-53A describes the specific conditions when security-related information can be reused in security authorizations, ongoing authorizations, and reauthorizations.

[73] Decisions to initiate a formal reauthorization action include inputs from the risk executive (function) and the senior information security officer.

or the common controls inherited by organizational information systems and explicitly accepting the risk to organizational operations and assets, individuals, other organizations, and the Nation. If the new authorizing official is not willing to accept the previous authorization results (including identified level of risk), a *reauthorization* action may need to be initiated or the new authorizing official may instead establish new terms and conditions for continuing the original authorization, but not extend the original authorization termination date. In all situations where there is a decision to reauthorize an information system or the common controls inherited by organizational information systems, the maximum reuse of authorization information is strongly encouraged to minimize the time and expense associated with the reauthorization effort.[74]

F.6 EVENT-DRIVEN TRIGGERS

Organizations may define event-driven *triggers* (i.e., indicators and/or prompts that cause a pre-defined organizational reaction) for both ongoing authorization and reauthorization. Event-driven triggers include, but are not limited to: (i) new threat/vulnerability/impact information; (ii) an increased number of findings, weaknesses, and/or deficiencies from the continuous monitoring program; (iii) new missions/business requirements; (iv) a change in the Authorizing Official; (v) a significant change in risk assessment findings; (vi) significant changes to the information system, common controls, or the environment of operation; or (vii) organizational thresholds being exceeded.

A significant change is defined as a change that is likely to affect the security state of an information system. Significant changes to an information system may include for example: (i) installation of a new or upgraded operating system, middleware component, or application; (ii) modifications to system ports, protocols, or services; (iii) installation of a new or upgraded hardware platform; (iv) modifications to cryptographic modules or services; or (v) modifications to security controls. Examples of significant changes to the environment of operation may include for example: (i) moving to a new facility; (ii) adding new core missions or business functions; (iii) acquiring specific and credible threat information that the organization is being targeted by a threat source; or (iv) establishing new/modified laws, directives, policies, or regulations.[75]

If a formal reauthorization action is initiated, the organization targets only the specific security controls affected by the changes and reuses previous assessment results wherever possible. Most routine changes to an information system or its environment of operation can be handled by the organization's continuous monitoring program, thus supporting the concept of ongoing authorization. An effective monitoring program can significantly reduce the overall cost and level of effort of reauthorization actions.

F.7 TYPE AUTHORIZATION

A *type authorization*[76] is an official authorization decision to employ identical copies of an information system or subsystem (including hardware, software, firmware, and/or applications) in

---

[74] The decision to initiate a formal reauthorization action can be based on a variety of factors, including for example, the acceptability of the previous authorization information provided in the authorization package, the length of time since the previous authorization decision, the risk tolerance of the new authorizing official, and current organizational requirements and/or priorities.

[75] The examples of changes listed above are only *significant* when they meet the threshold established in the definition of significant change (i.e., a change that is likely to affect the security state of the information system).

[76] Examples of type authorizations include: (i) an authorization of the hardware and software applications for a standard financial system deployed in several locations around the world; or (ii) an authorization of a common workstation or operating environment (i.e., hardware, operating system, middleware, and applications) deployed to all operating units within an organization.

specified environments of operation. This form of authorization allows a single authorization package (i.e., security plan, security assessment report, and plan of action and milestones) to be developed for an archetype (common) version of an information system that is deployed to multiple locations, along with a set of installation and configuration requirements or operational security needs, that will be assumed by the hosting organization at a specific location. The type authorization is used in conjunction with the authorization of site-specific controls (e.g., physical and environmental protection controls, personnel security controls) inherited by the information system.[77] The RMF tasks listed in Chapter 3 address the authorization activities associated with the employment of system-specific, hybrid, and common controls.

F.8 AUTHORIZATION APPROACHES

Organizations can choose from three different approaches when planning for and conducting security authorizations to include: (i) an authorization with a *single* authorizing official; (ii) an authorization with *multiple* authorizing officials; or (iii) *leveraging* an existing authorization.[78] The first approach is the traditional authorization process defined in this appendix where a single organizational official in a senior leadership position is both responsible and accountable for an information system. The organizational official also accepts the information system-related security risks that may impact organizational operations and assets, individuals, other organizations, or the Nation.

The second approach, or *joint authorization*, is employed when multiple organizational officials either from the same organization or different organizations, have a shared interest in authorizing an information system. The organizational officials collectively are responsible and accountable for the information system and jointly accept the information system-related security risks that may adversely impact organizational operations and assets, individuals, other organizations, and the Nation. A similar authorization process is followed as in the first approach with the essential difference being the addition of multiple authorizing officials. Organizations choosing a joint authorization approach are expected to work together on the planning and the execution of RMF tasks (see Appendix H) and to document their agreement and progress in implementing the tasks. Collaborating on the security categorization, selection of security controls, plan for assessing the controls to determine effectiveness, plan of action and milestones, and continuous monitoring strategy, is necessary for a successful joint authorization. The specific terms and conditions of the joint authorization are established by the participating parties in the joint authorization including for example, the process for ongoing determination and acceptance of risk. The joint authorization remains in effect only as long as there is mutual agreement among authorizing officials and the authorization meets the requirements established by federal and/or organizational policies.

The final approach, *leveraged authorization*, is employed when a federal agency[79] chooses to accept some or all of the information in an existing authorization package generated by another federal agency (hereafter referred to as the *owning* organization[80]) based on a need to use the

---

[77] Site-specific controls are typically implemented by an organization as *common controls*.

[78] Authorization approaches can be applied to both information systems and to common controls inherited by one or more organizational information systems.

[79] In this situation, federal agency includes any organizations that are subordinate to the agency. For example, NIST is a subordinate organization to the Department of Commerce.

[80] The term *owning* organization refers to the federal agency or subordinate organization that owns the authorization package. The information system may not be owned by the same organization that owns the authorization package, for example, in situations where the system/services are provided by an external provider.

same information resources (e.g., information system and/or services provided by the system). The leveraging organization reviews the owning organization's authorization package as the basis for determining risk to the leveraging organization.[81] When reviewing the authorization package, the leveraging organization considers risk factors such as the time elapsed since the authorization results were produced, the environment of operation (if different from the environment of operation reflected in the authorization package), the criticality/sensitivity of the information to be processed, stored, or transmitted, as well as the overall risk tolerance of the leveraging organization. If the leveraging organization determines that there is insufficient information in the authorization package or inadequate security measures in place for establishing an acceptable level of risk, the leveraging organization may negotiate with the owning organization for additional security measures and/or security-related information.[82] Additional security measures may include, for example, increasing the number of security controls, conducting additional assessments, implementing compensating controls, or establishing constraints on the use of the information system or services provided by the system. Security-related information may include, for example, other information that the owning organization may have discerned in the use or assessment of the information system that is not reflected in the authorization package. The additional security measures and/or security-related information may be provided by the leveraging organization, the information system developer, some other external third party, or some combination of the above.

The leveraged authorization approach provides opportunities for significant cost savings and avoids a potentially costly and time-consuming authorization process by the leveraging organization. Leveraging organizations generate an authorization decision document and reference, as appropriate, information in the authorization package from the owning organization. In situations where addition security measures are implemented, the leveraging organization documents those measures by creating an addendum to the original authorization package of the owning organization. This addendum may include, as appropriate, updates to the security plan, security assessment report, and/or plan of action and milestones. Consistent with the traditional authorization process described above, a single organizational official in a senior leadership position in the leveraging organization is both responsible and accountable for accepting the information system-related security risks that may impact the leveraging organization's operations and assets, individuals, other organizations, or the Nation. The leveraged authorization remains in effect as long as the leveraging organization accepts the information system-related security risks and the authorization meets the requirements established by federal and/or organizational policies. This requires the sharing of information resulting from continuous monitoring activities conducted by the owning organization (e.g., updates to the security plan, security assessment report, plan of action and milestones, and security status reports). To enhance the security of all parties, the leveraging organization can also share with the owning organization, the results from any RMF-related activities it conducts to supplement the authorization results produced by the owning organization.

For all three authorization approaches described above, risk management-related activities (including RMF tasks) involving external providers are carried out in accordance with the guidance provided in Appendices H and I.

---

[81] The sharing of the authorization package (including the security plan, security assessment report, plan of action and milestones, and authorization decision document) is accomplished under terms and conditions agreed upon by all parties (i.e., the owning organization and the leveraging organization).

[82] Negotiations with the owning organization may include other organizations (e.g., when the information system and/or services are provided to the owning organization in full or in part, by an external provider).

CONTINUOUS MONITORING

MANAGING AND TRACKING THE SECURITY STATE OF INFORMATION SYSTEMS

A critical aspect of managing risk to information from the operation and use of information systems involves the continuous monitoring of the security controls employed within or inherited by the system.[83] Conducting a thorough point-in-time assessment of the deployed security controls is a necessary but not sufficient condition to demonstrate security due diligence. An effective organizational information security program also includes a rigorous continuous monitoring program integrated into the system development life cycle. The objective of the continuous monitoring program is to determine if the set of deployed security controls continue to be effective over time in light of the inevitable changes that occur. A well-designed and well-managed continuous monitoring program can effectively transform an otherwise static security control assessment and risk determination process into a dynamic process that provides essential, near real-time security status-related information to organizational officials in order to take appropriate risk mitigation actions and make cost-effective, risk-based decisions regarding the operation of the information system. Continuous monitoring programs provide organizations with an effective mechanism to update *security plans*, *security assessment reports*, and *plans of action and milestones*. The following sections provide a general overview of some fundamental concepts associated with continuous monitoring. NIST Special Publication 800-137 provides additional guidance on the development and implementation of information security continuous monitoring programs.

G.1 MONITORING STRATEGY

Organizations develop a strategy and implement a program for the continuous monitoring of security control effectiveness. The monitoring program is integrated into the organization's system development life cycle processes. A robust continuous monitoring program requires the active involvement of information system owners and common control providers, chief information officers, senior information security officers, and authorizing officials. The monitoring program allows an organization to: (i) track the security state of an information system on a continuous basis; and (ii) maintain the security authorization for the system over time in highly dynamic environments of operation with changing threats, vulnerabilities, technologies, and missions/business processes.

Continuous monitoring of security controls using automated support tools facilitates near real-time risk management and represents a significant change in the way security authorization activities have been employed in the past. Near real-time risk management of information systems can be facilitated by employing automated support tools to execute various steps in the RMF including authorization-related activities. In addition to vulnerability scanning tools, system and network monitoring tools, and other automated support tools that can help to determine the security state of an information system, organizations can employ automated security management and reporting tools to update key documents in the authorization package including the security plan, security assessment report, and plan of action and milestones. The documents in the authorization package are considered "living documents" and updated accordingly based on actual events that may affect the security state of the information system.

---

[83] A continuous monitoring program within an organization involves a different set of activities than Security Incident Monitoring or Security Event Monitoring programs.

Timeliness is critical for near-real time risk management. Organizations are encouraged to consolidate available information into measures that can be displayed as trend reports or other types of dashboard visualization to assist decision makers with timely review and decision making. Transitioning to a near real-time risk management environment requires the increased use of automated support tools over time as organizations integrate these technologies into their information security programs in accordance with available resources.

An effective organization-wide continuous monitoring program[84] includes:

- Defining a continuous monitoring strategy based on risk tolerance that maintains clear visibility into assets, awareness of vulnerabilities, up-to-date threat information, and mission/business impacts;

- Establishing and implementing a continuous monitoring program that includes monitoring all implemented controls at the organization-defined frequency;[85]

- Analyzing and reporting findings to appropriate organizational officials;[86]

- Responding to findings with mitigation, acceptance, transference/sharing, or avoidance/rejection; and

- Reviewing and updating the continuous monitoring strategy and program to increase visibility into assets and awareness of vulnerabilities.

Continuous monitoring is a tactic in a larger strategy of organization-wide risk management. Organizations increase situational awareness through enhanced monitoring capabilities and subsequently increase insight into and control of the processes used to manage organizational security.

G.2 FREQUENCY OF SECURITY CONTROL MONITORING

The criteria for determining the frequency of security control monitoring is established by the information system owner or common control provider in collaboration with the authorizing official or designated representative, chief information officer, senior information security officer, and risk executive (function). The frequency criteria reflects the organization's priorities and importance of the information system (or in the case of common controls, the information systems inheriting the controls) to organizational operations and assets, individuals, other organizations, and the Nation in accordance with FIPS 199 or CNSS Instruction 1253. Organizations may use recent risk assessments (including current threat and vulnerability information), history of cyber attacks, results of previous security assessments, and operational requirements in guiding the frequency of security control monitoring.

---

[84] Although the primary focus of continuous monitoring activities is on the effectiveness of security controls employed within and inherited by an information system, there are other equally important external factors in the environment of operation for a system that also require monitoring on an ongoing basis. These factors include, for example, changes in the organization's missions or business processes, changes in the threat space, and changes in tolerance for previously accepted risks.

[85] Through the use of automation, it is possible to monitor a greater number of security controls on an ongoing basis than is feasible using manual processes. As a result, organizations may choose to monitor a greater number of security controls with increased frequency.

[86] Organizations have significant latitude and flexibility in the breadth, depth, and formality of security status reports. At a minimum, security status reports describe or summarize key changes to security plans, security assessment reports, and plans of action and milestones. At the discretion of the organization, security status reports on information systems can be used to help satisfy the FISMA reporting requirement for documenting remedial actions on any security-related weaknesses or deficiencies.

While a comprehensive discussion of considerations for determining monitoring frequencies is provided in NIST Special Publication 800-137, it is important to note that security controls that have the greatest volatility and the controls that have been identified in the organization's plan of action and milestones are typically monitored more frequently. Security control volatility is a measure of how frequently a control is likely to change over time subsequent to its implementation. For example, security policies and procedures in a particular organization may not be likely to change from one year to the next and thus would likely be security controls with lower volatility. Access controls or other (technical) security controls that are subject to the direct effects or side effects of frequent changes in hardware, software, and/or firmware components of an information system would likely be controls with higher volatility and therefore, require more frequent monitoring. Security controls identified in the plan of action and milestones are also a priority in the continuous monitoring process, due to the fact that these controls have been deemed to be ineffective to some degree. Such controls may also require more frequent monitoring. The authorizing official or designated representative approves the set of security controls that are to be monitored on an ongoing basis as well as the frequency of the monitoring activities.

G.3 KEY DOCUMENT UPDATES AND STATUS REPORTING

Continuous monitoring results are considered with respect to any necessary updates to the security plan, security assessment report, and plan of action and milestones, since these documents are used to guide future risk management activities. Updated security plans reflect any modifications to security controls based on the risk mitigation activities carried out by information system owners or common control providers. Updated security assessment reports reflect additional assessment activities conducted by assessors to determine security control effectiveness based on modifications to the security plan and deployed controls. Updated plans of action and milestones: (i) report progress made on the current outstanding items listed in the plan; (ii) address vulnerabilities discovered during the security impact analysis or security control monitoring; and (iii) describe how the information system owner or common control provider intends to address those vulnerabilities. The results of monitoring activities are reported to authorizing officials on an ongoing basis in the form of status reports. Other key organizational officials (e.g., risk executive [function], senior information security officer) receive the results of continuous monitoring activities as needed or as requested. With the use of automated support tools and effective organization-wide security program management practices, authorizing officials have the capability to access the most recent documentation in the authorization package at any time to determine the current security state of the information system, to help manage risk, and to provide essential information for potential reauthorization decisions. The monitoring of security controls and changes to the information system and its environment of operation, continues throughout the system development life cycle. Summaries of monitoring results are provided to the senior information security officer and the risk executive (function).

OPERATIONAL SCENARIOS

APPLYING THE RISK MANAGEMENT FRAMEWORK IN DIFFERENT ENVIRONMENTS

Managing risk to information from the operation and use of information systems in modern computing environments with a diverse set of potential business relationships can be challenging for organizations. Relationships are established and maintained in a variety of ways, for example, through joint ventures, business partnerships, outsourcing arrangements (i.e., through contracts, lines of business arrangements, interagency and intra-agency agreements), licensing agreements, and supply chain arrangements.[87] The Risk Management Framework (RMF) applies only to federal information systems. There are two distinct types of operational scenarios that affect how organizations address the RMF steps and associated tasks:

- Information systems used or operated by *federal agencies*;[88] and

- Information systems used or operated by *other organizations*[89] on behalf of federal agencies.

SCENARIO 1: For an information system that is used or operated by a federal agency, the system boundary is defined by the agency. The agency conducts all RMF tasks to include information system authorization. The agency maintains control over the security controls employed within and inherited by the information system.

SCENARIO 2: For an information system that is used or operated by *another organization* on behalf of a federal agency, the system boundary is defined by the agency in collaboration with the other organization and one of the following situations applies:

- If the organization is contracted to a federal agency, the contractor can conduct all RMF tasks except those tasks which must be carried out by the federal agency as part of its inherent governmental responsibilities.[90] The agency provides RMF-related inputs to the contractor, as needed, and maintains strict oversight on all contractor-executed RMF tasks. The contractor provides appropriate evidence in the security authorization package for the authorization decision by the authorizing official from the federal agency.

- If the organization is a federal agency, the organization can conduct all RMF tasks to include the information system authorization. The information system authorization can also be a joint authorization if both parties agree to share the authorization responsibilities. In situations where a federal agency uses or operates an information system on behalf of multiple federal agencies, the joint authorization can include all participating agencies.

---

[87] NIST Special Publication 800-53 provides additional guidance on the application and use of security controls in external environments to include relationships with external service providers.

[88] References to federal agencies include organizations that are *subordinate* to those agencies.

[89] Organizations that use or operate an information system on behalf of a federal agency or one of its subordinate organizations can include, for example, other federal agencies or their subordinate organizations, state and local government agencies, contractors, and academic institutions.

[90] Organizations ensure that requirements for conducting the specific tasks in the RMF are included in appropriate contractual vehicles, including requirements for independent assessments, when appropriate.

APPENDIX I

SECURITY CONTROLS IN EXTERNAL ENVIRONMENTS

PARTNERSHIPS, OUTSOURCING, AND SUPPLY CHAIN CONSIDERATIONS

Organizations are becoming increasingly reliant on information system services provided by external providers to carry out important missions and business functions. External information system services are services implemented outside of the authorization boundaries established by the organization for its information systems. These external services may be used by, but are not part of, organizational information systems. In some situations, external information system services may completely replace the functionality of internal information systems. Organizations are responsible and accountable for the *risk* incurred by use of services provided by external providers and address this risk by implementing compensating controls when the risk is greater than the authorizing official or the organization is willing to accept.

Relationships with external service providers are established in a variety of ways, for example, through joint ventures, business partnerships, outsourcing arrangements (i.e., through contracts, interagency agreements, lines of business arrangements), licensing agreements, and/or supply chain exchanges. The growing dependence on external service providers and new relationships being forged with those providers present new and difficult challenges for the organization, especially in the area of information system security. These challenges include:

- Defining the types of external services provided to the organization;

- Describing how the external services are protected in accordance with the security requirements of the organization; and

- Obtaining the necessary assurances that the risk to organizational operations and assets, individuals, other organizations, and the Nation arising from the use of the external services is acceptable.

FISMA and OMB policy require external providers handling federal information or operating information systems on behalf of the federal government to meet the same security requirements as federal agencies. Security requirements for external providers including the security controls for information systems processing, storing, or transmitting federal information are expressed in appropriate contracts or other formal agreements. Organizations can require external providers to implement all steps in the RMF with the exception of the security authorization step, which remains an inherent federal responsibility that is directly linked to the management of risk related to the use of external information system services.[91]

The assurance or confidence that the risk from using external services is at an acceptable level depends on the trust[92] that the organization places in the external service provider. In some cases, the level of trust is based on the amount of direct control the organization is able to exert on the

---

[91] If the external provider is a federal agency, the provider can conduct all RMF tasks to include the information system authorization (see Appendix H).

[92] The level of trust that an organization places in an external service provider can vary widely, ranging from those who are highly trusted (e.g., business partners in a joint venture that share a common business model and common goals) to those who are less trusted and represent greater sources of risk (e.g., business partners in one endeavor who are also competitors in another market sector).

external service provider with regard to employment of security controls necessary for the protection of the service and the evidence brought forth as to the effectiveness of those controls. The level of control is usually established by the terms and conditions of the contract or service-level agreement with the external service provider and can range from extensive (e.g., negotiating a contract or agreement that specifies detailed security control requirements for the provider) to very limited (e.g., using a contract or service-level agreement to obtain commodity services[93] such as commercial telecommunications services). In other cases, the level of trust is based on factors that convince the organization that the requisite security controls have been employed and that a determination of control effectiveness exists. For example, a separately authorized external information system service provided to an organization through a well-established line of business relationship may provide a degree of trust in the external service within the tolerable risk range of the authorizing official.

The provision of services by external providers may result in some services without explicit agreements between the organization and the external entities responsible for the services. Whenever explicit agreements are feasible and practical (e.g., through contracts, service-level agreements, etc.), the organization develops such agreements and requires the use of the security controls in NIST Special Publication 800-53. When the organization is not in a position to require explicit agreements with external providers (e.g., the service is imposed on the organization or the service is commodity service), the organization establishes explicit assumptions about the service capabilities with regard to security. In situations where an organization is procuring information system services or technologies through a centralized acquisition vehicle (e.g., government-wide contract by the General Services Administration or other preferred and/or mandatory acquisition organization), it may be more efficient and cost-effective for the originator of the contract to establish and maintain a stated level of trust with the external provider (including the definition of required security controls and level of assurance with regard to the provision of such controls). Organizations subsequently acquiring information system services or technologies from the centralized contract can take advantage of the negotiated trust level established by the procurement originator and thus avoid costly repetition of the activities necessary to establish such trust.[94] Contracts and agreements between the organization and external providers may also require the active participation of the organization. For example, the organization may be required by the contract to install public key encryption-enabled client software recommended by the service provider.

Ultimately, the responsibility for adequately mitigating unacceptable risks arising from the use of external information system services remains with the authorizing official. Organizations require that an appropriate *chain of trust* be established with external service providers when dealing with the many issues associated with information system security. A chain of trust requires that the organization establish and retain a level of confidence that each participating service provider in the potentially complex consumer-provider relationship provides adequate protection for the services rendered to the organization. The chain of trust can be complicated due to the number of

---

[93] Commercial providers of commodity-type services typically organize their business models and services around the concept of shared resources and devices for a broad and diverse customer base. Therefore, unless organizations obtain fully dedicated services from commercial service providers, there may be a need for greater reliance on compensating security controls to provide the necessary protections for the information system that relies on those external services. The organization's risk assessment and risk mitigation activities reflect this situation.

[94] For example, a procurement originator could authorize an information system providing external services to the federal government under specific terms and conditions of the contract. A federal agency requesting information system services under the terms of the contract would not be required to reauthorize the information system when acquiring such services (unless the request included services outside the scope of the original contract).

entities participating in the consumer-provider relationship and the type of relationship between the parties. External service providers may also in turn outsource the services to other external entities, making the chain of trust even more complicated and difficult to manage. Depending on the nature of the service, it may simply be unwise for the organization to place significant trust in the provider—not due to any inherent untrustworthiness on the provider's part, but due to the intrinsic level of risk in the service. Where a sufficient level of trust cannot be established in the external services and/or service providers, the organization: (i) employs compensating controls; (ii) accepts a greater degree of risk; or (iii) does not obtain the service (i.e., performs missions or business operations with reduced levels of functionality or possibly no functionality at all).